THE TIME & TREE

KATHLEEN OLSON

ISBN 979-8-88616-303-2 (paperback)
ISBN 979-8-88616-304-9 (digital)

Christian Faith Publishing
832 Park Avenue
Meadville, PA 16335
www.christianfaithpublishing.com

Printed in the United States of America

1320: THE NEWBORN

It was unusual. A lone man with all his possessions was staggering through the open prairie. His burden was light as his chattel included only a blanket, a pouch, a bow with some arrows, and a stone knife at his side. He wore a necklace of herbs, a bone, and some feathers that he had been given as powerful medicine for a hunter.

He stopped and sat in the high grass to rest. He hurt, even though he would never let anyone know. However, that wouldn't be hard since he found himself alone in the middle of big nowhere. He had no idea where he was or what he was doing out there. And why was he in so much pain? He made a quick inventory of himself and found he was covered in dry blood, the right side of his face was bigger than the left, his ribs jabbed with every breath, and his right arm felt as if the lower half of it had been cracked like an egg. He had no idea how this could have happened. He did, however, know what to do about his arm. Taking two of his precious arrows, he put them alongside his arm, pulled a few strands of the woven blanket out, and tied it around his arm, using the arrows as a splint. It was a hideously painful act.

He tried to get up off the ground, but he found that one-handed and hurting all over was too agonizing. So he sat. It gave him time to think. Where was he? Where and who were his people? Who was he? How did he manage to end up alone in the middle of such an empty world? How could he get help? He had no real answers even though the word *buffalo* kept bouncing through his brain, but why?

Eventually, he realized that he needed sleep more than anything. He managed to get his blanket and wrap himself in a way that didn't impede his already arduous breathing. Slowly, he lay down and positioned himself so the pain wasn't overwhelming. The noonday sun shone down, giving a lovely warmth to his battered body. And he slept.

Waking up was not pleasant. Everything hurt all over again, and it took him a few frantic moments to find the rhythm of his breath once more.

Hunger was his problem now. He knew that his pouch had been wrapped with his blanket, so he looked for it. The pouch was there, and he rifled through it. He came up with a handful of acorns, some dried corn, berries, and a nice stash of buffalo jerky. The jerky went well, but it made him thirsty. He had no choice but to look for water.

The soil on the treeless prairie was moist, black, and loamy, which told him that it was possible to find puddles. With a tremendous effort, he stood up, his ribs jabbing him and hampering his breathing. His arm dangled at his side and engulfed him in pain. His splints didn't do much of a job. Although from a distance the prairie looked flat, it was actually an undulating landscape. He walked to the crest of the nearest hill and was rewarded by a small puddle in a dip in the ground. Although he had to get down to it to drink, he did it with the same pain; but this time, he didn't notice it as much.

Refreshed by the drink, he also saw a large piece of bark. With no trees around, he wondered briefly how it got there. However, it was a gold mine to him, and he picked it up and broke it in half lengthwise using his good hand and one of his feet. The bark would save the arrows he needed and be a better splint. Again, he had to go through the process, but it was easier this time. He got up with much difficulty and began to walk, taking his blanket and bow.

As he walked, directionless, he began to sort things out. He remembered why the word *buffalo* was stuck in his head. He had been hunting buffalo, and it was summer. That was it! The summer buffalo hunt! But where was everyone else? Usually, the whole tribe…wait. What tribe? Who were they, and how would he find them? The word *buffalo* went even further in his mind. What was it? He remembered someone shouting the word at him. It didn't take long to put the two together. Someone shouted at him, so it could be his name. It came to him suddenly and easily. His name was Singing

Buffalo. In a flash, more things became clear. His people were the Pawnee, his wife's name was Moon Dancer, and he lived on the banks of the Kickatuus River.

He checked his position with the sun and easily found west. Since they usually went east on the buffalo hunts, that told him west was the direction of his village. He gathered his blanket, bow, and arrows and began to walk. It was a slow, tormenting walk, but a walk nevertheless. He tired easily and had to sit down or even sleep a bit before he could go on. Getting up and down was still a tortuous chore, but now he had a goal, a prize to find. Home.

The wind picked up, and Singing Buffalo looked at the western sky. A storm was coming. On the prairie, storms could be amazingly quick and terrible. There was no shelter. He flattened himself on the ground and waited. The rain began, and a splitting sound of thunder made his head hurt even worse. The wind was furiously sweeping in circles, lifting him off the ground. He felt every injury in his body scream, and he lost consciousness.

When he opened his eyes, he was cognizant enough to remember his situation. He also remembered how he came to be there in that condition. It was a sin to do what he had done. It was the summer buffalo hunt. He had done what he had only heard about: He didn't wait for the signal to attack the animals, went too soon, and spooked the whole herd. And for that act, the other hunters beat him. They must have beaten him badly enough so they thought he had died of it. He had heard this sort of thing happen, and, as a boy, he vowed he would never do that. But he did and ruined that day's hunting. So they left him there. However, they left him the dignity of his belongings in case he wasn't dead.

He finally decided that he had had enough for the day and sat down, gathering his blanket around him. Unanticipatedly, he realized he had left his pouch with his food in it at the place where he first found himself. So he was now without food, and he was in too much pain to try to go back. With his arm broken, it was impossible to use his bow, and the only weapon left to him was his stone knife in its holster by his side. There wasn't much of a chance to get food that way, and he didn't see any bushes around that might yield berries.

In due time, Singing Buffalo died, alone, still trying to get back to his tribe. He left behind his blanket, stone knife, bow, arrows, and, somewhere, the pouch.

Without the competition of other trees, as would be in a forest, and a skyful of sunshine, the oak sprout photosynthesized all it wanted. It was a beginning of a long, long journey that began in the wind that picked up the pouch and scattered dried corn, berries, and acorns across the prairie. But the secret of the beginning of The Tree would always be a mystery to those who followed.

1650: THE RITUAL

It was the break of dawn when Brown Owl heard the warrior running through the village singing. The voice was joyful yet pained, mixed with burdens. Brown Owl couldn't quite get the words of his song exactly except the last part when the warrior said, "I am seeking for you." The boy was curious as to what was going on, but he felt so warm under his calf skin blanket, cozy in bed with his grandmother that even trying to understand what was going on was something he could find out later.

In the usual manner, he was awakened by his father saying, "The fire is ready." It encouraged everyone to get up.

The earth lodge where he lived was a microcosm of his universe. Two extended families lived in it, and everyone had a place of their own as well as a place with everyone. Brown Owl's place was his bed with his grandmother, Northern Star, and next to them was his best friend, Loud Call, who also shared a bed with his grandmother. His father and mother, Sitting Bear and Walks-Like-Willow, shared a bed at the northwestern end of the circular lodge nearest the altar.

The first thing Brown Owl did in the morning after relieving himself was to run out the entryway and get a good look at the sky to see what kind of day was ahead of him. It was a normal spring day that he found that morning, and he was happy to see it. He and Loud Call always had plans. However, there were chores, and Brown Owl remembered he wanted to find out why the warrior was singing through the village so early in the morning.

During breakfast of corn porridge with strips of dried buffalo meat in it, he tried to get his father's attention, but he couldn't. Sitting Bear was in a deep conversation with his uncle, Walks-for-Long. He just wanted to find out what was going on.

It was after breakfast that Brown Owl was able to catch his father's eye.

"What is it you need, my son?"

"I just wanted to know why a warrior was going through the village singing this morning just before dawn."

"You said he went through our village singing?"

"Yes, Father."

"I must find out more. I'm going to visit More Corn."

Brown Owl was now completely confused. More Corn was the village priest. Whatever would his father and the medicine man have anything to do with the singing warrior?

It seemed the news spread quickly, and men from many families gathered with More Corn. Brown Owl was more and more curious. He watched as men gathered at More Corn's earthen mound, and when he had a chance, he advanced little by little until he was not three-antelope lengths from the gathering. He listened carefully, but with so many talking, he couldn't understand what one individual was saying.

He gave up but wanted to include Loud Call in his little adventure. Just as he was about to tap his friend on the shoulder, his father rushed in.

"We're going to celebrate the Morning Star ritual," he said to Walks-Like-Willow. He seemed excited, and his mother looked concerned.

"What is your part in it?" she asked.

"Those jobs won't be determined for a few days as Bent Tooth and More Corn will stay together for four days of prayers and planning."

"I hope you won't be part of finding the girl, especially if she would be Cherokee. You know how dangerous they can be."

"Woman, what is to be has not been determined yet. When it comes, I will obey."

"As you say," she answered.

While doing his chores, Brown Owl could think only of the singing warrior, Bent Tooth, and he desperately wanted to know what all the hubbub was about, why his mother looked so concerned, and why his father looked like he was about to go on a great adventure.

As promised, four days later, the men gathered around More Corn's dwelling, anxious to hear what was to be said. Brown Owl hid behind The Tree and listened.

"After four days of prayer and much thought, Bent Tooth and I have made some decisions."

The crowd seemed to gather closer, and Brown Owl was afraid that he wasn't going to be able to hear everything. He cupped his ear with his hand. More Corn held the sacred Morning Star bundle, and suddenly Brown Owl remembered what it was. The holy objects it held were Mother Corn, a pipe to be smoked and shared as tradition taught, a hawk skin, some downy feathers, an otter skin collar, an extra pipe, and a wildcat skin with its legs stuffed with tobacco. These things Bent Tooth would use to imprison the Morning Star. For four days, Bent Tooth, dressed in the holy objects, went through the village, asking men he knew were ready to help to come with him. Sitting Bear was asked to be his assistant.

The night before the men left on their journey to find the Morning Star sacrifice, More Corn and others, from midnight on, stayed up to watch for the Morning Star. When it appeared, the group of men began to dance. At the sight of the Star, the chosen men gathered and left on their journey.

Brown Owl had no idea what happened when they left what they were going to do, or how they were to do it. All he knew is that they would come back with a young girl from an enemy tribe who would be sacrificed next spring.

The boy slipped away from The Tree feeling shaken. This ceremony seemed so important and so steeped in tradition he could hardly believe anyone would be able to remember all the nuances.

Later in the morning, a group of boys Brown Owl's age were out with their bows and arrows shooting at a target pinned to The Tree. He grabbed his weapon and joined them.

"I didn't know anything about this practice. Who called it?"

"No one," Loud Call said. "We just thought we would practice in case one of us were asked to be 'the warrior' for the Morning Star ritual." That said, Loud Call sent off a volley of arrows directly at the target on The Tree, leaving permanent scars on the trunk.

Six days later, the warriors returned with a thirteen-year-old Cherokee girl who looked frightened and confused. She was taken to Knife Chief who would be in charge of her for the next year. She was bound and with him at all times and would even go on the summer and winter buffalo hunts.

Slightly troubled by the look on the girl's face and the conversation at the target practice, he sought his mother's council.

"Mother, I am troubled by the girl that Father and the other men brought back. Her only use seems to be her death. She must be very frightened. Does anyone even know her name?"

"I tell you truly, my son, do not trouble yourself with the girl. She is now holy and will nourish our crops and fulfill the promise of the Morning Star. She will be beloved by our tribe. But to know even her name will make it hard for you to see her killed next spring. She is helping us, and that's all you need to know."

His mother was right. All through the spring, he only saw her on rare ventures around the village. She was silent, downcast, and suddenly looked older than she did when she first arrived. With the winter buffalo hunt, Brown Owl saw more of her when the whole village went, but he was careful never to catch her eye. He wondered if she knew how valued she was by the tribe and was aware of her fate. As far as he could tell, she was treated kindly, even given her own bowl made of wood and a spoon made of buffalo horn. She was bathed and dressed, painted and pampered, but all the time watched by the keeper of the Wolf bundle.

That spring, More Corn watched the sky carefully for the return of the Morning Star. His vigilance was rewarded when the Star arrived in the sky ringed in red. It was time for the ceremony to begin. The ritual would be held in five days. Bent Tooth, as the visionary, was told to clear out his house as part of the ceremony would be held there.

Although Brown Owl was too young to be included in the ceremony in Bent Tooth's home, it didn't keep him away from listening. He heard singing and felt the ground shake from the dancing.

On the third day, More Corn gave directions for the sacrificial scaffold to be built. It was to be made to represent the four semicardinal directions, animals, colors, trees, and natural forces.

During the fourth day, the girl was taken out and her body painted red on the right side and black on the left representing night and day. All this was done while the singing and dancing continued in Bent Tooth's lodge until midnight. Then the singing stopped, and they began to proceed with the girl to the scaffold.

It was mandatory that each male in the tribe be in attendance. Brown Owl's mother said he had done this twice before, but he didn't remember. His mother told him that he was but a babe in his father's arms at his first attendance, and the second he was put in charge of his little brother, Rabbit. Brown Owl remembered that, but only that he had had to chase his brother all over to keep him safe and never really saw the actual ceremony. Now his brother was five years old and would stay where he was told. Brown Owl did as he was told and went to the ritual, taking his brother with him.

At the grounds about a mile away from the village, the girl was tied onto the sacred scaffold. Hidden from her was the chosen warrior who ducked out from the northwest with his bow and arrow and shot her through the heart. Brown Owl felt he also had been shot. He was almost on the verge of anger at having a life so wasted. Boys and men from the tribe came with their bows and arrows and riddled her body with their shots while singing war songs. Brown Owl refused to be any part of that even when directed by his father.

The girl's body was taken down from the scaffold, and her chest and abdomen were opened. She was taken about a quarter mile away and put on the ground, facedown to bleed into the soil as a renewal of hope and fertility.

The ceremonial earth lodge was opened, and all the people feasted on sacred buffalo meat. There was general rejoicing, and the music and songs took a different turn, songs of hope, joy, and giving thanks. People danced a different dance, and things took a turn. They started joking with one another, women especially found it funny to wear their husbands' clothes and poke fun at them. Everyone laughed, sang, and danced to exhaustion. Brown Owl, seeing that they were celebrating, seemed to change his mind. The girl had given the whole tribe hope as her blood blessed the ground and her soul kept the stars on track. And she was holy as his mother had said.

Brown Owl began to dance.

1782: THE FLIGHT

His name was Mio. He was running, walking, skulking, and hiding his way to the North. He wasn't sure where he was exactly, but in later years, they would call it Nebraska. All he knew was what the song said: "Follow the Drinking Gourd." Every night, he checked with the star-formed dipper, knowing the end of the handle was his ticket to freedom. But that was all he knew.

He didn't know where he was going to find shelter or food from day to day. He mostly just made a bed under the stars wherever he was. Taking a chance, he decided to cut through the countryside through the endlessness of the prairie rather than follow the haven the river and trees offered. Mio knew that if he was still being tracked, it would be sensible to be looking along the river. Besides, it was shorter through the prairie than along the winding river.

As for food, he had been lucky and bagged a pheasant the day before. Trouble was, there was no way to cook it without lighting a fire with telling smoke. Mio contented himself with anything he could dig up or find under a rock.

It was getting on to evening; the autumn cold was closing in, so Mio lay down in the high grass, said his prayers, threw his meager blanket over him, stuffed his nearly empty rucksack under his head, and slept.

The next morning as he walked, he saw faintly in the distance a thin green, red, and yellow line winding through the countryside. It was the river where it had gone around a bend. He thought he'd better go toward the river as he was about out of water. Picking up his gait to a trot, the closer he got, the more he noticed something else beyond the trees. It was a tan and green blob that he couldn't make out. He didn't think it could be a white settler as there were none that he knew of out this far west. His curiosity was piqued, and he hurried his pace.

The sun was directly overhead by the time Mio got to the river, his black skin soaked in sweat. The canopies of the trees shouted their vivid fall colors, and Mio reveled in their beauty. But he had to jerk himself away from his admiration and get down to business. He drank as much water as he could hold and filled up his canteen. He sat down on the riverbank and let his tired feet dangle in the cool flow. He was almost ashamed of himself for indulging in such a luxury. Almost.

Along with the water, Mio hoped to find something to eat at the river. He was in luck this time as there was an abundance of bushes loaded with their fall crop. Mio picked as many berries as his rucksack would hold.

Probably the main thing he was in search of was a place to hold up for the winter. Any place he could think of would be too obvious. If he were lucky enough to find a cave, that would be the best. But he didn't see any signs of such a feature.

Mio had to move on, and he was anxious to see what that tan blob was on the other side of the river. He found a wide expanse in the river with a sandbar rising up prominently, marking it a shallow place to cross. He began to wade into the current when he turned his head and looked south along the river. Men and horses. All of Mio's confidence drained out of his soul, and he stood stark still in the water for a moment until his sense of flight kicked in.

It wasn't going to be the end of him! He ducked back into the trees so quickly that the trees and bushes scratched his face and chest. If he stayed in the underbrush the river afforded, he might go unnoticed. He found a large, thick bush and tried to get to its interior, but it was thorny, and Mio was badly scratched and punctured. But he kept trying and stayed absolutely still when the men on horses came near.

Although Mio couldn't see out of the bush very well, he was puzzled at what he did see. The men were not white; they were more his color but with a lot of red mixed in. Their ponies didn't have saddles like he was used to seeing on his master's ranch; in fact, they rode bareback. The men had feathers in their hair, and they carried bows and a quiver of arrows.

Mio watched as their horses ambled by, and all three of the men were in a deep conversation. Mio couldn't understand a word of what they were saying. His eyes followed them as far as he could from the bush, then he came out, hid behind a small berry bush, and saw where they went. He was amazed to see that the tan-and-green blob about which he had been so curious was an Indian village, and it was crawling with people. After seeing that, he was surprised that all he had seen were those on horseback that passed him.

It didn't take Mio long to realize that he couldn't camp out on the river that night, not with the village so close. He had heard horrendous things about what Indians do to white people. He didn't even want to imagine what they would do to a black man.

Mio checked the riverbank where the three men rode and saw indications that this was a well-traveled path. Gathering his possessions and stuffing them in the bag, he began to walk back the way he came, but the scratches and stabs he received from the thorn bush slowed his gait. He managed to get away from the river and out into the grassy prairie, but he realized he was too much of a standout, and he dropped into the grass. But not quickly enough. He saw the three men that had passed him on the river riding swiftly toward him. There was nowhere to go, so he stood up and waited for them. He would meet his death on his own terms.

The horsemen circled Mio and shouted at him. One of them came close, put out his hand, and ran it across Mio's chest. The man looked at his hand then showed it to the other two. Two of them slipped down off their horses, and, without a fight from Mio, tied his hands together in front of him with a piece of leather string. Mio was allowed to walk, not dragged, behind the horses. He was astonished the Indians were so gentle with him. It was almost as if they were so curious about his skin that they wanted to take care of him.

When they got to the village, they dropped the tether, but Mio's hands remained tied. Immediately, he was surrounded by people of all sorts. He realized that these Indians had never seen a black man before. He was therefore touched all over his back and chest. Yes, they found, he was really black, and not a white man in disguise.

Finally, he was taken to a large mound with an entrance. He was led inside, but he was much taller than the Indians, and he had to duck. He was shown to a mat on the floor, and they indicated he was to sit on it. There they took off the leather thong that had held his hands prisoner. Before he could get a word out, an old man and a young woman came in. He began chanting something, and she knelt next to him and applied some kind of salve to his cuts and scratches. The soothing effect was almost transforming. He could see these people didn't want to harm him. They may even see him as good medicine.

For several days, he remained in the lodge. He wasn't without company as it seemed everyone in the village wanted to touch his skin. He allowed the impingement and even smiled when a mother brought in her baby. Mio touched the baby and made a silly face at it, and the child laughed. He was beginning to get a kick out of the children, but he couldn't help feeling like a sideshow to the adults.

He had a desperate need for communication with his hosts, but there wasn't anyone who spoke even rudimentary English. So he decided he would have to learn a bit of their language. One of the three Indians who had brought him into the village was a frequent visitor. Mio pointed to himself and said his name. The Indian did likewise, but Mio couldn't pronounce it as it was as long as his name was short. They connected, however, by way of pantomime, and Mio quickly learned the names for various animals, how to say *thirsty*, *hungry*, and *sleep*. And best of all, he learned his captor's name and the English translation, Seeking Frog. The Indian pantomimed a boy hunting frogs then pointed to himself. Mio had no idea how he was going to explain his name.

That night, as every night had been, he was given a meal. He had recognized the buffalo, deer, or fish they had given him previously, but he just couldn't pinpoint the rather odiferous offing they had for him that night. He tried it, and surprisingly, he actually liked it once he could get around the smell. Later, Seeking Frog came to see him, so Mio, using his hands to talk, asked what the meat was. Seeking

Frog pantomimed a hunter, holding his nose and clubbing something. Then it came to him: the meat was skunk. Then he noticed Seeking Frog was smelling rather strong himself, and Mio saw a fresh skunk skin around his neck. Seeking Frog acted very proud that he had killed the skunk they both had had for dinner. Mio wanted to be sick.

In the days that followed, Mio was allowed out of the lodge. It took a while to get his sitting down muscles to unkink. The autumn day was glorious with a strikingly blue sky framing the bright autumn-ness. Almost immediately, the villagers congregated around him, but it seemed they had had their fill of touching his skin. Mio was rather relieved.

Since Mio had not even tried to get across the meaning of his name, there was a great interest in what to call him. Seeking Frog made a point of asking for it. So Mio did his best to pantomime *slave*, cruelty, and running away. Seeking Frog still looked puzzled until a woman came forward and indicated she knew what he was talking about. Seeking Frog's whole demeanor changed. He actually, in front of the whole village, approached him with sympathy in his eyes and hugged him. He indicated that several of their women and children had been captured and made into slaves. They had no idea how to rectify the situation or even where they were, but he hoped they would find the opportunity to also run away. From that time on, he was known as Long Run.

But the question kept coming up: What did *Mio* mean? Why was he called that? It involved an explanation that he couldn't translate. It wasn't long until he noticed that same woman who had informed Seeking Frog what Mio was trying to pantomime. He approached her, and she looked terrified and ran. Later in the day, he found Seeking Frog and asked him about the woman. Would she be able to understand better than the others what he was trying to say? And why did she run away from him? The reply was simple. Her name was Little Bird, and she had for a while been a captive of Sioux and had learned their language by pantomime. She ran because she was a young woman and was not supposed to have anything to do with men not approved by her family.

That was easily remedied. Mio asked Seeking Frog to introduce him to her family, smoke a pipe, and talk, even with gestures, with them. It wasn't long before the family was happy to have Little Bird try to communicate with him. So Mio and Little Bird became friends, and they began to understand each other's language with their hours of *talk*. She sympathized with Mio for his captivity and he with hers. She got the idea of what his name meant, and why it was hated by him.

Seeking Frog, Mio, and Little Bird got together once she had a good handle on what to explain. She said that Mio's name was given to him by his master, and it meant *mine*. Here, he belonged to no one and wanted to make his name belong to Long Run only. He would not belong to anyone again. He also had Little Bird explain to Seeking Frog that Long Run needed a tree to point the way for others that may come that way. He had bent many trees so they were pointing north, showing the way. But out on the open prairie, there were no trees. By the river, there were too many trees, and his pointed branch would be lost.

After a few moments of thought, Little Bird tried to explain what Seeking Frog said. She indicated that a tree grew not far from the village, but it was an old tree that he may not be able to bend. She would take him there, though, if he wanted. He wanted very much to do just that.

The next day proved to harbor nasty, rainy weather with strong wind gusts, but Long Run wanted to go anyway. Little Bird, wrapped in a blanket, met him at the edge of the village, and they walked, Mio guessed, about a mile north.

They were right. It was a tree, right in the middle of the prairie. How it got there was anyone's guess since it was not of the same oak family that grew along the river, and there were no other oaks around.

Yes, The Tree was somewhat old, and the branches were set, unmovable. But as he watched the tree in the wind, he saw one branch that was being blown around, and it looked quite supple. He headed for The Tree and inspected the branch that was waving about and found that it was, indeed, bendable. He knew he couldn't do it alone, so he asked Little Bird to be of help. Together, they moved the branch back and forth, breaking fibers inside so it could bend. When it did, he had the branch pointing outward due north. It could easily be spotted by anyone passing.

The winter was spent with the Pawnee. Now Long Run, living in the pleasant enclosure of his lodge surrounded by new friends, was content. He had marked the route that he had taken and was ready to go again in the spring.

In later years, that straightened branch became a favorite place for children to play. It also afforded someone seeking solace, or even as a secluded bench for young lovers.

Long Run made it to freedom. As he promised, he had marked the trail wherever he could. As he grew older, he settled in a town not too far from his last bent branch. He worked in a general merchandise store content with his lot. Every once in a while, he was asked to translate for a Pawnee who had wandered into the wrong territory. He was happy to feel that language in his mouth again and always thought of Seeking Frog and Little Bird. He himself was known as Charley Long Run. Mio was gone, and Charley was free.

1818: THE WEDDING

There was no doubt. Drusilla was truly in love with John. She and her mother had so many hostile conversations about the subject that both of them lost the reason for the argument. All Drusilla knew was that she loved John, and when he proposed, she felt she couldn't get the *yes* fast enough. John had even talked to her father before asking her, and he graciously gave permission, but her mother was opposed to the whole idea.

"You're too young."

"But, Mother, I'm seventeen now. It's time I settled down."

That was the basis of their argument.

"You have your whole life to settle down. As for now, I want you at home with me."

"It's not like you're alone," Drusilla reminded her again. "You have the other children and grandchildren. You surely won't be alone. And you have Father."

At this point, Mother would generally break into tears, and that would be the end of their words. To Drusilla's way of thinking, she had only one option.

John had a good farm on the other side of the mountain from her place in what one day would be West Virginia. They had met at a church social, and they both felt a pull toward each other almost immediately. Drusilla never understood the reason, but her mother took a dislike to John right away. She said he was born on the wrong side of the mountain, and "her people" didn't have anything to do with people from the other side.

Drusilla thought that was ridiculous. And when she had the nerve to say so, she risked getting further into the argument and both shedding tears. She usually kept quiet.

Her father was different. He liked John and was also baffled why his wife was against the people from the other side. And he told his daughter that.

"Father," Drusilla said tearfully, "if Mother won't let me get married, I'll do something I said I would never do. I'll get married to John without her there."

"That would break her heart."

"She's breaking my heart right now! I love John, but I want Mother to be happy too. This is just tearing me apart."

"Your mother told you she didn't want you to marry John for a reason I don't understand. But you, you were a little scamp as a child, and maybe it's time to be a scamp for one last time. Go ahead and marry John if he's the one who makes you happy. I'll tend to your mother."

John and Drusilla were married under an old oak tree in front of John's house. Her father did just what he promised and her mother was present—weepy, but present.

Four years later, John and Drusilla were the parents of two daughters, Nancy and Susannah, and she was about to have her third child. They were happy to be in their snug cabin in the mountains of Virginia, but the inclines were not conducive to farming. One noon, John came in from the fields banging the dust off his hat on his arm.

"That's it! I've had it!"

"John, whatever is wrong?"

"That's the third time this week I've fallen out of my cornfield!"

Drusilla looked helplessly at her husband. "What is there to do about it?"

"We pack up and move to the west where I've heard the land is flat."

Drusilla was horrified. "Leave Virginia? Leave my whole family? I want our children to know their grandparents, aunts, and uncles. Once we leave here, we may never see them again! Oh, John, isn't there any other way?"

"Not unless you can take a shovel and even off the mountains."

And so the little family packed up, said goodbye, and left Virginia. It took months for them to reach "just the right spot" that

John was looking for. Drusilla had no idea how he would know it when he saw it, except it would be flat. Flat was everywhere, and there were no trees except by the rivers and streams. But John knew his land. It wasn't far from the Platte River in the Nebraska Territory not far from Fort Kearney. And, to her surprise, off in the distance was a huge old oak tree, all alone, almost hidden by the uneven terrain.

While Drusilla set up housekeeping on the windswept prairie, she made a note that since there were no mountains, so there was no "other side of the mountain" people. She wondered what her mother would think of that!

John got busy with the building of their sod house since there were no trees with which to make a wooden house quickly. It took him weeks to make it, but it was summer, and they didn't mind camping in the covered wagon. John just wanted the little family to be covered before snow covered the land.

During this time, Drusilla gave birth to her first boy, and they named him Henry. John was out of his mind with delight to have a son.

By early fall, the soddie was up, and the family moved in. It took Drusilla a long while to get used to little bits of sod dropping over everything including the baby. He didn't seem to mind, but Drusilla became fanatical about the dirt in her clean house.

By January 1824, Drusilla realized another baby was on the way, and she felt the soddie, as it stood, was just not adequate for their burgeoning family. She had a long talk with John about adding on to the dwelling.

"I was going to start hauling trees from the riverbank to make a proper house," John said.

"But the riverbank is ten miles away if it's an inch," Drusilla reminded him.

"Do you want a wooden house or not? I'm sure you don't want to keep cleaning up like you do now."

"How long will it take to get enough lumber to build this house?"

"A long time. Can't say exactly."

"What about the crops? If you spend all your time on a house, we'll have no food for the winter." Drusilla mourned.

"I can handle both," John said. "After all, I don't have to take breaks from falling out of my cornfield any longer."

Having heard that the Nebraska Territory was treeless, John brought saplings with him: those from their home in Virginia and those he dug up on the way to their new home. He wanted a wood lot, but until the saplings were grown, they would rely on buffalo chips, which were abundant, for fuel.

John had particularly eyed The Tree in the distance, but Drusilla felt akin with it and insisted he wipe out of his mind anything he might want to do with it.

"We must leave it as it is. It's a beautiful old tree, and I am very fond of it."

That spring, magically, the fields were made ready for planting, the saplings were planted properly, and the logs from the river's edge came rolling in. Also, that spring, her second son was born. She named him Achilles.

John was never left without something to do. He was up at dawn and usually didn't get to sleep before midnight. The workload became a threat to his health. Drusilla, busy with the children and her own garden, was unable to help him as much as she would have liked. It appeared that they would be staying in the soddie for another winter. She didn't mind that since it was snug in the cold winter. The children, all but six-year-old Nancy, were too young to help. Drusilla sent Nancy out on buffalo chip hunts. Nancy apparently didn't mind because she always got a special treat when she came back with a basketful of chips.

Much to Drusilla's dismay, there were no real neighbors. With all the land, any neighbors were too spread out to find, and John always had the wagon. Once in a while, a curious Indian would ride onto their land. Drusilla forgave them for their lack of manners when they would come barging into the house without as much as a knock. The Indians scared her, so when one made an appearance, she was quick to bring out cornbread and tea for the *guest*. Soon, though, the visits became almost routine, and she began to recognize repeat guests. She lost her fear of these visitors as they were just curious, but she did wish she could communicate with them. She was able to give them her name by using overemphatic gestures and a loud voice. They promptly returned the gesture with their names, though Drusilla didn't understand what they said and certainly not how to pronounce them. She found that nodding and smiling got her further than any other method of communication.

In the spring of 1825, Drusilla had her fifth child, another boy they named John Jr. The wooden house was mostly done, but John just couldn't go on without help. So he took the wagon and went to Fort Kearney to see if they could help locate a neighbor or two. The soldiers were very helpful and pointed him in the direction of a well-worn wagon path.

"Just follow them tracks, and you'll find the Nelson house, and beyond that is the Dawson place. Both families had teenage sons that can help you raise that roof of yourn."

Drusilla was delighted at the news. She had no other adult to talk to other than John for the past two years, and she was hungry for that kind of companionship. When John brought the Nelson and Dawson men to help with the upper floor and roof of the house, they brought their wives and daughters, and a tableful of food. It was a party! When the dancing began, even the babies clapped their hands and laughed.

"Isn't it odd," John said that night as they went to bed, "that those families came over to help us with the house and yet not a lick of work was done?"

"Too bad we didn't get to know them better sooner. I had such a good time! It was heaven to see other females over the age of eight in the house. I wonder why we haven't met with them before?"

"Probably because their houses are in gullies in the hills. You just don't know the house is there until you come right across it. Besides, they all live about a mile north of The Tree, and we live a mile south. If it hadn't been for the soldiers, we never would have met. And, for your information," Tom Nelson said, "there was a church starting near the fort, and we'll meet lots of people there."

"A church? Oh, John, how I've missed that so! What time do we have to be there? How many other families are there going to be? Will it start this Sunday?"

"To answer your questions: ten o'clock, five, and yes."

It was hardly what she had remembered from her childhood. There was no white steeple building, only a dusty tent and some benches. But she had missed church so much that it didn't matter what the surroundings were.

It was also a magnet to unwelcomed guests. The Pawnee were very curious about the white man's doings, and this large tent was something that had to be investigated. The group of three Pawnee boldly walked into the tent, ripping the flap as they strode in. They laughed as they pointed at the destroyed doorway. Drusilla didn't know what to do. At home when a lone warrior came into the house, all she needed to do was give him something to eat and send him on his way along with the last of whatever baked goods she had. These men were nothing like that. Using their own language and pointing to the altar area, the families understood that they were to gather at the front of the church.

By this time, there had been enough witnesses that a posse was brought together and surrounded the tent. With the frightened people inside and the Pawnee, aware of the extras outside the tent, they lit a torch and tossed it to the torn doorway. Drusilla was aware that the tent would go up in seconds, along with the people and the Pawnee themselves if something wasn't done. Drusilla, being a small, compact woman, dove for the tent skirt and pulled as hard as she could until there was enough room for her to roll under and out. Others followed, but the fire burned itself out when the tent was gone, and most people suffered only minor burns. The Pawnee fled past the flames and rode away before the posse knew they were gone.

From then until winter, church was held under The Tree. In the meantime, the fellowship established a schedule that would allow each family to host a service. As more heard of the church, the more houses they scheduled into their service. Talk of a permanent building was always on people's minds, but nothing was ever done about it.

In the spring of 1827, Drusilla gave birth to a girl, Mary. Mary was not a well child from the start and died within a year. She was buried in her father's wood lot next to their house.

Between 1828 and 1836, five boys were born: George, Silas, Harrison, Levi, and William. John built on more house, and he put on a large room on the second floor to act as a dormitory for their bulging family. Again, there were the neighbors to help with the roof. John, in turn, spent many days helping with other construction projects along with the women and children who brought the food and the party after the day's work.

"With all the new help these five boys we have, we won't even need to have a bunch of neighbors give up their days to help us out," John observed.

"Now, John, they're only babies. George helps me around the house, and he loves to feed the chickens. Silas and Harrison try to *help* George, but that's about as far as help goes. We'll have to wait a few years before carpentry comes into the picture."

By the end of 1857, four more children were born: Drusilla Jr., Aaron, Brookie, and Thomas. This, Drusilla reasoned, would keep her busy even though so many of her children had grown, married, or gone off. Nancy and Susannah had married and, with their husbands, had left for California. She knew, like her own mother, she would never see them again.

John was always busy. Although it developed that being on the south side of The Tree was not the most desirable place to live, the community still admired and respected John for his hard work and generous nature. And remembering the prejudice being on the *wrong* side of the mountain created, he was determined to have some kind of an equalizer that would bring the two sides together as often as possible. Dances, church, and fairs were wonderful, but she realized that there was only one thing that would bring harmony to the area and be able to show Drusilla how precious she was to him, especially after fifteen children and almost forty years of marriage. This would have to be a special event, something that the people of the community had never witnessed before.

After that, Drucilla began wondering just what was going on with John. He started bringing things into the barn that she had never seen before. One thing looked like a table or a dresser or some such thing. But when she went to investigate, there was nothing there. Then he would ride out sans explanation only to come back an hour later with a pleased smile plastered on his face.

Church was crowded that spring day in 1858, and the bunch Drusilla and John brought with them always added to the crunch. They were meeting at Brian and Carla Doohan's that Sunday, and it wasn't unusual for the host family to supply dinner, but there was something in the air that Drusilla couldn't put her finger on, and extra table that made it look like a festival. She saw other women looking at her then giggling. She checked her apron to make sure she hadn't spilled something obvious on it. Her curiosity and suspicious nature were in high gear.

As dinner was being served buffet-style, people weren't exactly tearing into their food. In fact, they were simply standing around holding their plates. Finally, the other ladies came in from the kitchen and filled their plates too, but all eyes seemed to be on her. John had a beaming smile, one she had never seen before, and suddenly, he handed someone his plate, dropped to one knee, and took hold of her hand.

"Drusilla," John said with total adoration and excitement on his face, "we've been together for almost forty years now, and I think it's time we showed everyone how much we mean to each other. Drusilla, would you give me the honor of becoming my wife again?"

There was a deafening silence. Slowly John reached into his pocket and drew out a small box which he opened and offered to her. Inside was a ring with three stones, a garnet with an opal on each side that glinted in the candlelight.

"I couldn't afford this the first time around. Will you wear it now?" he said, almost pleading.

Holding out her hand, John slipped the ring on her finger. She held it up. She had never seen anything so pretty. She looked at John and nodded.

Almost scaring her to death, the people in the room let out with a whoop! There was going to be a wedding! *But when and where?* Drusilla wondered. *And how?* But John allied her fears.

"We'll be married on our fortieth wedding anniversary under The Tree, and we'll invite the whole town!"

It wasn't her habit, but Drusilla began to cry. She was confused at how much she had to do for a wedding, what she and the other children would wear, how could she be a hostess and the bride at the same time, and so many other thoughts that she thought her brain would pop.

"And you don't have to worry about anything," John said wiping her tears. "All the details have been taken care of. I had your old wedding gown altered, all the kids will have nice clothes thanks to the many hands in this community, and the wedding feast will be courtesy of everyone in town. All you have to do is something I don't think I've seen you ever do: relax. It's about time others did for you."

Drusilla was in awe, confused, and exhilarated all at once. She hadn't seen John be publicly romantic since their wedding in Virginia in 1818. But what had he been doing with all that was hiding in the barn, wearing that smug smile, and finally going down on one knee? It wouldn't take her long to find out.

It was May 16, 1858, their fortieth wedding anniversary, and there was Drusilla, just as confused, but totally euphoric about the whole idea. She dressed in her wedding gown, a blue number that was so much out of date that it almost embarrassed her. All the children were dressed in a similar color. John, knowing the tradition, kept out of sight.

To get to The Tree, Drusilla and the younger children were driven by Susan and Ben Jacobs, a couple from the north side of The Tree. The wagon was decorated with paper flowers and streamers. The older children were driven by another neighbor in a similarly decorated wagon or rode horseback. They looked like a parade.

The Tree itself was decorated agreeably like the *parade*, and Drusilla could see many, many people waiting beneath the sheltering boughs including some curious Pawnee Indians, some of whom she recognized as visitors to her home. She stepped down from the wagon and looked at what she rightly thought was the whole community, north and south siders mixed in a beautiful assortment.

Her oldest son, Henry, came to meet her, offered her his arm, and walked by to the edge of the congregation that parted creating an aisle to The Tree. Beneath it, she could see the *table* or *dresser* that John had hidden in the barn. It was an altar. Then she saw John, dressed in the same suit he wore on their wedding day, and there was the preacher, the Reverend Phelps. In spite of all the things that were vying for her attention, she saw only John.

They repeated the same vows they made forty years ago, and in the end, every spectator cheered when they were again pronounced married.

The party began right after the ceremony and lasted into the night, north siders dancing with south siders, kids, who couldn't care less about north or south, danced with one another. People mingled with people, ate, drank, and got to know one another. John could see, through his love for Drusilla, there was a hope that there would never again be a *wrong* side of the mountain in their community.

1860: THE RIDER

Gil didn't like reading much, and he hadn't gone to school long enough to be any good at it, but he was glancing at a discarded newspaper he found on a bench in town when he saw the notice: "Wanted: Young, skinny, wiry fellows not over eighteen. Must be expert pony riders willing to risk death daily. Orphans preferred."

After Gil's parents died in a Nebraska Sioux attack when he was only six, he was sent with a few other boys from the orphanage to live with a group of men who rounded up wild horses, tamed them, and sold them at auction. He was given good food and a place to sleep and nothing but horses to think about. Somehow, some schooling was squeezed into the cracks in his mind, and he did learn a bit of reading and some arithmetic enough to count the horses. He was put to work, hard work, and he loved it. Being around the horses was all he cared about, and by the time he was ten, he was doing most of the gentling when the men weren't around. He also learned to ride like there was a tornado at his back.

With help, he replied to the ad; and a few weeks later, he was contacted to go to Dobytown for an interview. Dobytown was only six miles away, so he walked since he ironically didn't have a horse to ride. Mr. Waddell, the interviewer, asked a number of questions about his present mode of living, the demise of his parents, and would he be willing to risk death every day.

"Oh, heck," he replied to the interviewer. "I don't have no one to come home to, and I'm itchin' to get out and see something of the country, especially on the back of a speeding horse. I grew up with them, and I would always bet on the loyalty of a horse before the loyalty of a man any day."

"All right, young man, you are now a Pony Express rider," Mr. Waddell said, shaking Gil's hand. "I can tell you'll be an asset to the organization. Report to me in one week. In the meantime, make sure your affairs are in order and get lots of rest. Good luck."

With what he had been told swimming around in his head, he turned back to the ranch. When Gil got back, he told the men what had happened. Every one of them clapped him on the back or punched him in the shoulder while telling him how much he would be missed and what a good job he had done over the years. They all took up a collection and handed him a total of eight dollars, more money than Gil had ever seen before.

Gil really didn't know what Mr. Waddell had meant by his *affairs*, but he did know the meaning of rest. He slept almost the whole week through with wake time spent with the horses and eating as much as he could.

He had mentioned to the men that he was told the Pony Express wanted to buy horses.

"I think," said one of the men, "that when you go to report for work next week, I'm going to talk to this man who hired you. Lord knows we've got plenty of horseflesh to sell. Maybe they'll be interested in our stock."

Gil was delighted. He might even be riding ponies that he had gentled himself.

When it was time to go, they gave him a pony to ride to Dobytown, and one of the men tagged along to not only bring the pony back but also to do some bargaining.

In the meantime, Gil peeked inside the Pony Express station. It was small and cramped, and each station had a manager who was responsible for the horses and making sure the rider was rested and fed before going on the next leg of the fifteen hundred miles to the West Coast. At each station, he would receive a respite, food, and a new horse before continuing his flight. In order to make the ride lighter, all correspondence he carried was written on tissue paper.

He found that the Pony Express riders wore a uniform of the company's signature red shirt and blue pants. He also had to take an oath not to drink, swear, or fight with any employees. Each rider was fitted with a gun and given a Bible.

Just as he was finishing up his inspection of the station, a sound of hooves in a fury came to a halt at the station door. A rider hopped off, and the station manager left his bargaining to fix the bone-weary rider some chow and let him sleep while he cared for the horses.

"Okay, Gil, it's your turn. This man's been riding since St. Joe, Missoura, and he's done for now, but the mail has to keep on going. Slip on the mail pouch and then come with me, and I'll show you where we keep the stock."

Anxiously, Gil tagged along around the back where there was a barn and two horses. "We could use a few more mounts. Glad you brought your friend with you. I think we'll do business. Now, get on your horse and head to the next station that's twelve miles away, and you'll need to go as fast as you can. But remember, this is Pawnee country, and them Pawnee don't like white people on their territory, even the ones just passing through."

That was the only thing Waddell had said that made Gill uncomfortable. The Pawnee weren't the same as the Sioux who had killed his parents, but they were still Indians.

Gil nodded and mounted a pinto. It seemed used to riders as it started to run before Gil could signal. He was momentarily surprised at the pony's strength and willingness for velocity.

This is what he loved! This is what he had waited for! Going faster than any of the horses he had tamed, the wind tore at his face, and the dust peppered his eyes. It was all he could do to keep his hat even though he had tied it on. It was glorious! And, in no time it seemed, the twelve miles had melted away, and the next station was in sight. He reluctantly pulled on the reigns to make the flying pony stop. When he dismounted and stretched his legs, he was handed a bit of food before he grabbed the next pony handed to him by the station manager, and took off. He didn't think there was anything better in the world.

After several stops, Gil was fed a watery beef stew that was not terribly filling but very tasty, and he had three bowls of it. Picking up the precious mail pouch, he was off again on a fresh mount.

Each rider was responsible for fifty to one hundred miles per trip, but Gil wanted to keep on going even with night falling, and he had no light. So he did the next best thing: He stopped at his last station and immediately went to sleep.

The next day, he was up at dawn and ready for a run. He was put on an Appaloosa. When this run was through, he found himself in Laramie, Wyoming, more than two hundred miles from where he started out in Dobytown.

The station manager approached him the next morning and told him he would be headed east on his next leg.

"Why? I thought I was going to be going all the way to California."

"Since you're new, we have to break you in a bit before you tackle the mountains. It's a confusing trail, and you'll need someone to talk you through it. We do this for every tenderfoot, so don't feel put upon. Besides, you easily passed your trial run. When you go back, you'll end up at St. Joseph, Missoura. Everyone starts there sooner or later."

That meant Gil had to go back much farther than Dobytown. He still got a rise out of going as fast as he could on the willing horse, but when his ride ended, he found St. Joe was a busy place which made him uncomfortable. He was used to the soft solitude of the open prairie. The Pony Express had its own facilities along the bustle of a busy city. He met with a man named Strange Eye who was part Pawnee, part Sioux, and part white. It didn't take long for Strange Eye to school Gil in the mountain paths.

"Don't even think of straying off the paths," Strange Eye warned. "You could easily end up over a cliff."

That did not bring a pleasant picture to Gil's mind. But he still had time to study the map Strange Eye gave him since he wasn't scheduled to go out for another day yet.

It was several days later when he crossed the line back into Nebraska with Fort Kearney his next stop. His mount that day seemed a bit skittish, but Gil had enough time with spooked horses, for he was sure he could control it. In spite of the horse, he urged the animal on for as fast as it could go.

It was just a snake. He had passed hundreds on his journeys, but this mount wasn't having any of it. It put on the brakes without warning, and for the first time in his life, Gil was scared. He flew over the top of the horse's head and smacked into a huge, old oak tree.

In an undetermined time later, Gil opened his eyes. The horse was gone, and the sun was making its way toward a fiery sunset. He tried to move, but a huge bolt of pain hit him in his leg and hip. He looked around to nothing. No one or nothing was anywhere, and so was he. He had no food or water and no way to move. He looked at The Tree that had stopped his flight and saw a red blotch on it, just about where his lower extremities must have hit The Tree. He looked down at his blue pants, and they were covered in blood. Obviously, he had broken a bone or bones. On inspecting his leg as best he could, he saw the ripped pants and an object sticking through.

Then it started to rain. But that was a good thing, Gil thought. At least he thought he would have water. But The Tree was too sheltering and the rain fell outside of his reach. Whatever did manage to get through the canopy was scooped up in Gil's hand before it hit the ground. It still wasn't enough.

As he lay there, he tried to break through the pain and get his thoughts together. Sooner or later, he realized, someone would be coming along that trail, possibly another Pony Express rider. They would find him, and he would get help. He just had to wait. That was something that was almost impossible given the pain he was in. In spite of himself, he drifted into unconsciousness.

Morning was well on its way to noon by the time Gil's foggy senses could make out his surroundings again. And still, the pain remained.

But there was something else in the picture once his view was completely clear. There was someone sitting just to the side of him. He had been found! Trying to look more closely, it was a surprise and a bit of a scare to realize it was an Indian who had found him. He thought, *Lord knows what he'll do to me.*

The Indian noticed Gil was trying to move, but he put his hand on Gil to signal him to stay still. Gil recoiled mentally from the Indian's touch. Gil put his hand on his throat and coughed to indicate he was thirsty, a gesture that was understood. Gil tried to communicate with him in English, but the Indian, that he recognized as Sioux, appeared to know very little.

When the Indian got up to go get the water, Gil noticed that the man's shoulder dipped down with every other step. He had a wooden leg. This prompted Gil to dub him "Half Leg." He indicated his own name by pointing to himself and slowly and loudly pronounced "Gil." Half Leg smiled, pointed to himself, and said his name in Sioux. Gil couldn't understand or pronounce it, so he pointed to himself and said his name. Then he pointed to the Sioux and said, "Half Leg." The Indian smiled and repeated it.

Half Leg signed that he was going to go for help of which Gil could only understand a bit of, but he nodded, and the Sioux took off leaving the water behind for Gil.

It was way past noon when Gil heard hooves approaching. Hoping it was another Pony Express rider, he tried to twist his neck toward the sound. That seemed to be the one physical thing he could do without pain.

Surprised, he saw it was Half Leg coming with two other men and one woman. One of the men spoke broken English, so after a quick exchange of names, he found that one of the men's names was "Good Fire" and the other he couldn't understand. The woman, however, could pronounce her white name, and it was Bright Morning. She had come on a pony that was dragging something, and Gil could see it was a travois. Gil realized they were going to take him somewhere, and he had no idea how he would survive the pain.

The nameless man looked at his leg and touched the thing sticking out of his leg. He turned to Gil and said something in Sioux, and Bright Morning said, "Bone out." The thought of it made Gil a bit sick. This prompted him to give the Indian the name "Doc Sioux."

Doc Sioux gave Gil a plant to chew on, and immediately his mouth went numb. He gladly accepted more of the plant that Doc Sioux offered until his whole body felt like his mouth. Somehow the group of Indians got Gil onto the travois. Gil felt the pain, but he no longer cared.

Much to his surprise, he didn't go to the Indian's village, but instead to Fort Kearney, some miles away. There they found the army doctor and left him there. Gil never got to say thank you.

Gil stayed at Fort Kearney for several months. Although he could no longer ride for the Pony Express, he worked hard after he had healed to get back on a horse. It would never be the same since he couldn't go any faster than a trot. He knew he would walk with a limp for the rest of his life so he took the Indian name "One Step." It was the only way he could think of to honor and forgive the tribe that rescued him.

1865: THE TOWN

Since The Tree was old and large, it became a point of reference for passersby on the road that formally had been used by Pony Express riders. Once they saw The Tree, they knew they were half a day's ride to Fort Kearney, but it had been a wearying trek from their jumping-off point that morning, so more and more people camped around The Tree, and some just decided to stay.

At first, it was an area of scattered tents and lean-tos; but finally, one bold soul constructed a soddie. Then another. According to the preemption law of 1841, a house had to be built on the land within thirty days, or they would lose the 160 acres that went with it. Instead of farming, one man decided to open a blacksmith shop, and another enterpriser built a saloon. It wasn't long before there was a general store, a dry goods, a feed and grain, a cobbler, and a bank. Later came the church and the school and many other small businesses. That number of establishments seemed to be just fine for the people of what would later become an actual town in years to come.

The Pony Express, now forgotten with the advent of the telegraph, left its trail that was followed by men on their way west to find a new life. A scant few now and then decided that the would-be town was to their liking, so they stopped for a while, and a traveler or two might decide to stay.

Finally, the town was in need of law enforcement as the one saloon had expanded to five. There were fights every night, and these had the local gentry up in arms, and there was no way to stop it. So the now full-fledged town had an election, and a sheriff was determined. Unfortunately, he was killed in the second bar fight he tried to stop. Another election, another sheriff. He did a little better before he was permanently disabled a few weeks later.

This time, the town wasn't going to squander another sheriff. So when election day rolled around, not only was a sheriff called to duty, but the sheriff himself appointed deputies. That seemed to calm some of the saloon crowd, and the sheriff, after inspecting the bars, decided that three of them had to go. Two of them were nothing but fronts for illegal activities and the other was so filthy that when the sheriff asked for a shot of whiskey, there was a fly and scum floating in it. Those closings really cut down on the fights each night.

The town finally had a town council that voted on laws. The sheriff insisted that any new saloon be inspected for activities that shouldn't be allowed and also for cleanliness. It was a radical idea, but the town council went along with it. The council also voted to no longer allow travelers to camp around the big oak tree that marked the start of their town. The Tree had become the focus of the town, and they decided to make that land into a park. They had a local carpenter build benches around The Tree so the citizens could enjoy the shade and serenity The Tree brought.

The town grew slowly but at a rate that the populace was able to keep up with itself. By 1900, the old Pony Express route had become a highway into town, and it saw its first horseless carriage that year. Most of the town came out to see the wonder, but horses on the street were terrified and bolted. One family on a wagon was tossed into the street when their horse tried to run and made a sharp turn too quickly. They weren't hurt badly, but their wagon was a loss. This prompted the sheriff to ask the council to pass a law that if anyone was going to bring a horseless carriage, or automobile as some called it, into town, the driver must display an artificial horse's head on the front of the machine. It did help calm the local equines, so the law remained on the books for the next thirty years. By that time, no one even had a horse head, much less displayed one, and the automobile population vastly outnumbered the horse.

The park with The Tree was a local gathering place. Older men sat on the benches while young mothers sat with their backs against the ancient tree trunk as they watched their children play. Permanent checker and backgammon boards were painted onto tables built for the park, and over in the corner was a slide, some swings, and a tee-ter-totter. It was really a place for everyone.

By 1960, the saloons that plagued the town in its infancy were long gone. They had been replaced by *pubs*, local bars, or even a family-friendly restaurant. There were drunken fights now and again, but they were taken care of by the local constabulary. Gone were the sheriff and his deputies and replaced by a police force. The town council still existed, but now it was presided over by a mayor.

Franchises had become evident. The town bragged a chicken joint, a burger nook, and an ice-cream franchise. They were all in the square that was built around The Tree. For a while, littering had been a problem as burger wrappers as well as litter from the chicken place and the ice cream parlor continued to blow around the square. Then the council realized there wasn't a trash can anywhere around The Tree, so they quickly obtained the vessels, and by in large, the trash problem was solved.

So many of the buildings that were built in the early days were gone or transformed. One of the saloons was now a hardware store, and the blacksmith's shop was a gas station. Wanting to preserve the history of the town where possible, the gas station owner had taken the original building and used its boards to make the interior of the station look like the old shop with the station franchise clearly marked on the outside. The owner of the hardware store liked the idea so much that when the rest of the original building had to come down due to expansion, he took those boards and lined one of the interior walls with them.

The one schoolhouse had come down as it was a fire hazard. In its place were three elementary schools, a junior high school, and a high school. The football team named themselves, "The Mighty Oaks."

The old generic church was gone with five others in its place. Presbyterian, Lutheran, Catholic, Methodist, and a synagogue. As they were all grouped within the same area, people referred to the neighborhood as the "religious shopping center."

The populace thought of The Tree as the heart and soul of their town, and indeed it was. No one knew how old it was, but experts guessed it was at least five hundred years old. It was there and theirs. Just standing near it, one could feel the age and certain wisdom considering how much this tree had seen and would continue to see.

1870: THE BUCKET

Milford wasn't stupid. He had actually graduated from high school, something most people around the town couldn't brag. But Milford didn't brag about anything much. He had as much as other people did, but he read everything that came his way such as newspapers, magazines, books, flyers, or even campaign posters. As long as it had print on it, he'd read it and remember it. Sometimes he wished he could forget some of the things he had read. He said it clogged up his thinking and messed up his talking. No, Milford wasn't at all stupid. He was just a little henpecked.

He was in town that morning looking for several things for his wife. One was a bucket. He headed to the general merchandise store and found a cluster of others ahead of him. Easing his way through the crowd murmuring, "Why are these people here on a Tuesday morning?" He found what he was there to purchase. He held up the bucket so John, the owner, could see and made a scribbling motion in the air indicating for him to put it on his account. John nodded and imitated Milford's scribbling motion.

Why Louisa needed to have a bucket from the store instead of homemade was beyond him, but she ruled the household. He did as he was told.

When he got home, he set the new bucket by the outdoor pump so Louisa could inspect it. It wasn't half an hour later when she came steaming out to the chicken house where Milford was cleaning.

"There's a hole in the bucket," she announced.

"What would you like me to do about it, Louisa dear?"

"Take it back to John and tell him he sells defective merchandise."

Milford knew he couldn't do that. John was an old friend, and Milford wasn't about to insult him. He'd take it back, but only to see if he could exchange it. So he hitched up the team and drove it into town.

By the time he got there, the crowd had subsided, and he was able to talk to John. When he explained what happened, John shook his head.

"Sorry, Milford, but you got the last bucket in the place. I won't be getting another shipment of those for at least a month. Why don't you just make a bucket like most people?"

"Louisa wants store-bought. I haven't a clue why."

Leaky or not, Milford kept the bucket for the time being. Maybe it could be patched, but it was better than no bucket.

He took his problem to Will, his hired man of many years. He was fairly sure Will could come up with a solution. But Will inspected the faulty pail and shook his head.

"I can see this thing leak," Will agreed, "but I don't see from where. It looks tight to me, but there she blows, leaking down the side from some crack other or another. I'm afraid I would have to take the whole thing apart, tighten the staves, and put it back together to make it work."

"That seems like an awful lot of work for a stupid bucket. Can't you make one? Oh, no," Will stopped and reminded himself, "Louisa wants it store-bought."

"I suppose you could go down the way to the Carlson's. They make everything themselves: buckets, barrels, casks, kegs. If it's round and has staves, they make it. It would be just like store-bought."

"No, that wouldn't be honest. Can you take it down there and ask Rafe if he would have a look at it, and can it be salvaged?"

"I guess I could. He owes me a bunch of favors anyway."

Will rode out with the defective bucket, but he stopped halfway by The Tree, took out a smoke, and enjoyed it under the sheltering branches. He always took time to spend with The Tree when he went through town. But his horse was getting restless, and he didn't want to spend too much time to make his employer suspicious about his unscheduled stop.

Rafe Carlson was an older man who had three sons who stayed to work the land with him. Each boy had a quarter of the claim, and each worked their own fields and, in turn, raised and harvested their father's portion. When Will told Rafe what he wanted, the man roared with laughter.

"You mean you can't figure out why it's leaking or how you can fix it?" Rafe thought that was very amusing, and when he told his sons, they had their chuckle too.

"Why don't you just buy one of ours?" Rafe asked. "We make 'em good and tight."

"Louisa wants a store-bought one. I don't ask. I just do as I'm told."

Two of the boys, Henry and Sedge, were sure they knew what to do.

"Just get some straw, stick it in the leak good and tight, and then shellac it," Henry advised.

"I can't pinpoint the leak," Will confessed.

"Let me have it," Sedge said confidently. "I'll take care of that detail." He went around the side of the barn with the bucket and came back a few minutes later.

"You're right. I can't find it either."

The third son, Jed, grabbed the bucket and said, "There isn't a leak I can't find. Of all the buckets and kegs and stuff we make, I've never produced leaky one." He took the bucket into the barn. Everyone heard some banging noises, and Will was afraid he was taking the thing apart. If that was the case, he'd have to stop at The Tree and smoke at least three before he could go home.

Jed came out looking confident. "I found it. And it's not just one place, it's several. That's why it wasn't easy to find." He held up the bucket, looking a little worse for wear, and showed them the cracks in the staves.

"Why don't you just take it back to John? It'd be a lot easier than trying to repair it."

"I tried that," Will said, "but John said he wouldn't have a shipment in for a while, and we need a bucket now."

"I'll bet," Jed said, "if I could get some birch bark and get it into the cracks, it would seal them. The Indians use birch bark on the canoes after all. But I don't know where to get birch bark out here."

"Why don't you ask Sitting Bear?" Henry asked. "He's usually in town. Since he married that white woman his tribe won't have much to do with him."

"Good idea," Jed agreed. "Let me have that bucket, and I'll take it with me. I'm going into town this afternoon anyway."

Will gladly handed the bucket over. On the way back to the homestead, he stopped at The Tree and smoked four.

Jed wasn't sure if he would run into Sitting Bear that afternoon, but he walked by the Princess' Palace saloon anyway. He was in luck.

Sitting Bear's English was good even though he stumbled on a few words. When Jed told him the problem with the bucket, Sitting Bear laughed much like Rafe had when Will first came to him with the problem.

"I was thinking birch bark would be the best to stuff in the cracks," Jed said.

Sitting Bear agreed. "Where are you going to get birch bark?" the Indian wanted to know.

"I have no idea," Jed admitted. I thought you might know since your people use it to cover your canoes."

"We use hides, not birch bark. Can't find any birch bark in this part of the country. The only tree here is The Tree in the square."

Jed was stumped. He couldn't go back to Will and admit failure. He'd have to keep looking. His eyes roved over the town, and they fell on the carpenter's shop. Since most people on their claims were carpentry smart, Jed had not had any reason to go into the establishment. This was the time to get to know the owner.

After introductions were made, Jed explained the reason for the visit. The carpenter chuckled. "What you need is some good oak, cut very thin, of course, to ease into the cracks. That would do it. I can give you some shavings."

Jed gladly took the shavings, thanked the owner, and left the shop. Then he thought, *How am I going to get those fragile shavings into those tiny cracks? Would there be anyone in town who would be capable of getting that done?* Then he thought of the jeweler.

"Well, and why not," he said out loud. He walked to the shop and found it locked. He knocked on the door. A small man with an eye loupe over his head finally answered. He looked suspiciously at the bucket Jed was carrying.

"What can I do for you, young man?" the jeweler asked warily.

"I have a silly thing to ask, but I don't know who else to go to."

"Oh, I've been asked silly things before. Please come in."

Jed complied and thanked the little man. He introduced himself and found that the jeweler's name was Daniel.

"Now what can I do for you, Jed?"

"I need to get these shavings into the cracks in this bucket. The tools I have are much too big. Could I ask if I could borrow some of your tools to get that done? I told you it was a silly request."

"I don't lend my tools out, but my son is a woodworker, and he has a set of small tools for delicate woodworking. Why don't we ask him?"

In a minute, Dan Jr. appeared and look at Jed then looked at the bucket. When he understood what his father was asking, he laughed.

"That's the same reaction I've had from everyone!" Jed said with some frustration. "Can you do anything with it?"

When Dan Jr. asked why he didn't just buy a new bucket, Jed explained.

"Okay, I'll give it a shot. Give me a few minutes."

It took almost an hour for the process to finish. Dan Jr. came from the back and said, "It was a challenge, but your shavings are now in those nasty cracks. If you soak the cracks, the wood and the shavings will expand and plug the holes."

Jed thanked him, paid him for his time, and went back to the spread.

On the way home, Jed stopped at Milford's and handed the bucket off to him.

"How did you end up with the bucket?" Milford wanted to know.

"If I can remember right, you gave it to Will, Will took the bucket to my dad, Dad gave it to Sedge who handed off to me, and I took it to town. In town, I took it to a carpenter, then to a jeweler followed by the jeweler's son. It's been a long day, and Will owes me ten cents for what I paid Dan Jr. for his work. But what you need to do now is to fill the bucket with water and let the shavings swell. Then you'll have a bucket, but it has to be soaked first."

Milford proudly took his new bucket back to his wife and told her to draw water from the well and fill the bucket so it could soak before it would be usable. Louisa's comment was straightforward.

"I can't do that."

"Why not, Louisa?"

"There's a hole in the bucket."

1871: THE SAPLINGS

Fort Kearney was no longer a viable asset to the United States government, so they simply closed it. This had a sorry outcome for several burgeoning towns across the area like Buda and Dobytown. They also became unnecessary and disappeared back into the prairie.

When Jake and Carla Hilliard arrived in the area, they were sad to notice that there were no trees in Nebraska except for the ones along the Platte River that were old cottonwoods and burr oaks. They claimed their property according to the Land Act and began planting their own trees, fruit saplings of all kinds. It was a joy to see them growing, and he urged his neighbors to do the same.

A man named J. Sterling Morton felt the exact same way as Hilliard and decided to do something about it. After much work, Mr. Morton signed a document in December of 1871 for April 10, 1872, to become what he called Arbor Day. It was simply a day to help turn the vast prairie into a tree-lined Eden. And it worked! More than a million trees were planted that day.

Unfortunately, with the exit of the soldiers at Fort Kearney came lawlessness. The abandoned land left by the fort was lush, green, and inviting to the herdsmen who started to move their cattle into Nebraska from Texas. Although there were cowboys who were supposed to keep cattle on abandoned land, they let them wander.

Cattle are not known to be light-footed, and when they wandered, it was onto farmers' land where the crops were eaten or trampled. Jake Hilliard's fruit saplings were victims. Like the other farmers who had fallen victim to the cowboy's negligence, they screamed and demanded payment for the damages. They were ignored by the cattlemen.

Tempers grew razor-thin, and by 1874, the rumblings of a storm were clearly heard by the town. As more and more drovers came from Texas, the cowboys got bolder, and more crops were ruined, sometimes along with buildings. When the cattlemen came into town and drank at the saloons, it didn't take long for them to find a reason to shoot up the place.

At one point, the cowboys rode through town shooting at random. Three bullets went into The Tree, and a fourth knocked some bark off. Those scars would remain with The Tree the rest of its life.

By that time, the townspeople were furious. An organization was formed to put a stop to all the shootings, especially after a man crossing the street was designated as the target for a group of cattlemen. The man escaped serious harm, but it only infuriated the townsfolk more.

Three of the most dangerous men were identified, all from Texas. They were Hank Merrill, his brother Marv, and someone named Victim. The serious shooting began when Marv Merrill took a shot at the marshal. Townsmen converged on the scene to help the marshal, and before the shooting ended, a cowboy named Cappy had been killed.

When Victim fired a shot into a saloon a few days later, hell was let out of the bottle. Fortified by a few drinks at the saloon, a group of about twenty-five herdsmen headed toward the marshal's office. The marshal promptly ordered them out of town. With the addition of the extra cattlemen, it was about even, herders to townspeople.

Backing off toward the railroad tracks, the cowboys could see the townspeople were ready for a battle; and this time, the townies were organized. During the battle, Hank Merrill was shot in the abdomen and then clubbed. It didn't take him long to die.

Seeing that one of their leaders was down and another wounded, the cowboys found refuge on an island in the Platte River. They still threatened the town saying they would burn it down as soon as reinforcements came from Texas.

The town, however, decided to take measures that nothing like that was going to happen. They drilled every day next to the railroad depot and soon were ready for battle. Some of the townspeople wanted to storm the island where the cowboys were holed up, but others insisted on waiting for them to leave. A twenty-four-hour guard was posted around the town so there would be no surprises.

In spite of the ruckus that was part of the town's growing pains, what was left of the trees planted that day in 1872 flourished in the soil of Nebraska. Each year, more were added. By 1920, they had the largest orchard in the Midwest. Every tree strengthened the town with its growth, and the townspeople knew they would never need to go back to the days of Hank Merrill and Victim. The town had grown up with the saplings solidly backed by The Tree.

1875: THE RIDE

Some people thought of Jim Raymond as a man just looking for an opportunity, and others didn't think anything of him at all. He kept to himself but had a habit of asking about the financial situations of others in the town. Most people found that rude and wouldn't give him any information while he did manage to extract a few bits from some.

After a couple of months of nosing into other people's business, he quite disappeared. The majority of the town didn't even notice, but Sheriff Ben Landry kept his ear to the ground. There was something just not quite right about Jim.

About a month after Jim had dropped out of sight, Mary Harper started asking questions about Amelia Goodrick and her three daughters. She reported that she hadn't heard from her in a long time, and when she went to the house, she found none of the Goodricks at home but strangely ran into Jim Raymond.

That was enough for Ben, and he took off for the Goodrick ranch to see what was going on and what Jim Raymond was doing there. He pulled up to the ranch as Jim was gathering livestock and the wagon and about ready to pull out.

"Mornin', Jim. What are you doing here?"

"Mornin', Sheriff. Mrs. Goodrick gave me a job looking after her ranch while she was waiting for Frank to come home from prison."

"And you seem to be doing a clean sweep of it. Whatcha you doing with Mrs. Goodrick's horses and wagon?"

"She got tired of waiting for Frank and decided to pack up and go back east where her folks are. She asked me to take her horses and sell them and pay her debts."

"Where is Amelia now, Jim?"

"Prob'ly halfway to Boston by now," Jim replied with half a smile on his face.

"Guess that means you're out of a job. Whatcha going to do next?"

"Been talking with Purlie Murphy. I'll bunk with him for a while. Then I'll just see what comes up."

"Well, good luck," the sheriff said as he turned to go to his horse. Something was wrong. His answers sounded like they had been rehearsed, and they were too pat. There was nothing to do now but wait.

True to the plans he told the sheriff, Jim moved in with Purlie Murphy and, in fact, struck a bargain with him to take over part of his ranch for all the work he would do around the place. Purlie was breeding appaloosas, and Jim knew that people would pay a good dollar for the staying power of the smart and speedy horses.

About a month later, the word came around to Sheriff Landry that no one had seen Purlie Murphy in a couple of weeks. It was time to pay a call at the Murphy ranch.

It was déjà vu when Ben got to Murphy's. There was Jim with a string of appaloosas about to leave the ranch.

"Whatcha doing this time, Jim?" the sheriff shouted at him. When Jim turned his head to look, he had what resembled the appearance of a frightened deer, but that quickly turned into an oily smile.

When Jim got his wits about him, he replied, "I'm taking this string over to the Sumner Ranch. They bought them."

"That looks like everything. What's Purlie going to do for breeding stock? Where is Purlie, anyway?"

"Aw, he had an errand, and he'll be back in about an hour."

"Then," Ben said, "I'll be back tomorrow. I'm anxious to talk to him about a few things."

"Okay, Sheriff. See you tomorrow." Jim turned and began taking the horses east, which the sheriff thought was odd because the Sumner Ranch was to the south. A close eye had to be put on this ranch.

Come to find out the next day that when Jim took the horses east, he didn't stop. When Ben got to Murphy's ranch, it was abandoned. All the stock was gone, the front door was open, and, when he looked inside, all the furniture was in place just like it was waiting for Purlie to come home. A quick ride over to the Sumner Ranch clinched his thinking: Jim Raymond was a horse thief. That alone was a hanging offense. And with a lack of Purlie Murphy and Amelia Goodrick and children also missing, the sheriff was experiencing a hollow feeling in his gut. It was time to get a posse together and find these people.

There was no lack of people to volunteer for a posse. Purlie was easygoing and well-liked. No one really knew the Goodricks except for a few of their neighbors, but that didn't stop men from wanting to help.

Like Purlie's ranch, the Goodrick place was abandoned, all the furniture in place. Ben peeked in the kitchen and the bedroom and noticed that all things were still in situ that no woman would travel without. Ben started looking around with a keen eye to see what else didn't make sense. Then he noticed the fireplace. It was a normal fireplace except the slabs of rock in front of it were a bit askew, and one was tipped.

Ben and some of the posse lifted the stones up, dug a little deeper, and sadly uncovered the bodies of Amelia's two older children, Molly and Susan.

"Okay, men, it appears we're on the trail of a murderer as well as a horse thief. But there are two more bodies to find. You three"—Ben pointed to the three Payton brothers—"go into the cellar and see if you notice anything, and I mean anything, out of place. The rest of us will go out into the pastures and see what we can find."

About an hour after the search started, one of the Payton brothers called to the others in the fields.

"Come on into the cellar. I think we found something."

When the posse got there, they explained that they had moved everything in the cellar and found nothing out of the ordinary. Then they noticed that the dirt in the center of the room was fresh, which was hard to determine in the cellar's gloom.

"So," said Jay Payton, "we moved the new dirt, and this is what we found." He pointed to the cellar floor, and there was a barrier of flat stones, almost like what was found in front of the fireplace. Sadly, they dug up the slabs, moved the rest of the dirt away, and found Mrs. Goodrick and her baby, Sally.

"This is what I was afraid of," Ben told the crowd. "It proves Jim Raymond is a thief, liar, and a murderer."

"Then as soon as we find him, we'll just string him up!" someone in the back said. That idea captured the entire group except for Ben.

"No one is going to string anyone up. Besides, we have no idea where to look for Jim, but when we do find him, we'll bring him back in for a fair trial."

There were shouts of disapproval. "Do you think he gave these people a fair trial?"

"He deserves to be hanged."

"What do you mean, Sheriff? He's the worst kind of scum."

"Horse-thievin' looney doesn't deserve anything fair."

Ben tried to calm the group before it became a mob. "Gentlemen, there is nothing that can be done right now. We have no idea where he is, and he got a day's start ahead of us. It may take a long time, but we'll find him."

The crowd simmered down, mumbling to one another.

"We still have to find Purlie Murphy," Ben pointed out. "Let's go to Purlie's ranch and see if he is there. We know what kind of burial to look for."

It didn't take them long to find Purlie in a corner of the north pasture buried in the same way as Amelia Goodrick's family.

Two years later, they were still looking for Jim Raymond. There were wanted posters out on him, but they didn't have any pictures, so it didn't do much good. Ben, however, stayed on the case. One of his first stops was the railroad station in a town about twelve miles away. It was two days after the posse had discovered the bodies. When the twelve-o-five arrived, he cornered the conductor and described Jim. He was no help, but the brakeman said he had seen him, and he had a ticket to Ohio. The sheriff thanked him profoundly and left.

This proved to Ben that Jim's escape was going east to melt into the crowds instead of the west where, with no cities to hide in, he would be in plain view.

One clue led to another, and it was finally determined that Jim Raymond, under the name of Andrew Kylie, was living in Cleveland. Ben had telegraphed Jim's description to the local constabulary, emphasizing Jim's huge, bushy beard. Ben was on his way to Cleveland. The town heard of his mission, and the muttering began. It would take several days by train to get back to Nebraska.

Ben found Jim locked up in a local jail having been accused of stealing a woman's wealth. Ben thought she was lucky to just lose her money. Knowing Jim, it would have been natural of him to murder her also. She kept her life and got most of her money back, but Jim was bound for judgment.

Between the time the town heard that Jim Raymond was in custody and was coming back for trial, and the day he was supposed to arrive, the muttering mob got nasty, then out of hand. They were all ready at the depot to welcome Jim and the sheriff with a rope and an ornery attitude.

Ben's deputy, Matt, was in the middle of the ruckus and knew it would be a bad scene all around if he didn't do something. He ripped off a telegram to the station he knew Ben and Jim would have to change trains:

"Mob building with rope at depot."

Ben sent a telegram back to Matt right away.

"Send Millie to next station with buckboard."

It was about an hour later when the train stopped at the next station. Millie, Ben's wife, was waiting. She was wiry, fast with her temper, and didn't like to lose at anything. Ben told her that the ugly crowd at the station at home was ready to string up Jim as soon as they got there, but if he wasn't on the train, that would solve the problem. However, she must get Jim to the jail before the train pulled into the station. Could she do that? Ben asked.

"Nobody is going to hang this piece of garbage out to dry when I'm there."

They fastened his cuffs, so Jim was tied by his feet and hands in a spread-eagle position in the seat behind the driver. He couldn't move, and that suited Millie just fine.

She whapped the reins over the backs of the horses, and they jerked the buckboard into motion. She slapped the reins harder, encouraging them along. Jim was terrified.

Millie looked over her shoulder and saw the train coming, gaining on her. She knew she had to be in town first and get Jim in the back door of the jail before the mob realized he wasn't aboard the train.

She and the train paced each other for a mile or so before Millie turned off into the prairie to take a shortcut. Unfortunately for Jim, who was being bounced around unmercifully, things were about to get a whole lot rougher. The prairie is anything but a smooth ride. With uneven ground, gopher holes, grass tufts, and, worst of all, buffalo wallows, there was no getting around fluidly. Jim held on as well as he could with his limbs shackled.

The first time she hit a gopher hole, the whole wagon bucked and became airborne. It slammed into the ground with a jaw-jarring crack, and he yelled at Millie to slow down! But that only seemed to spur her on as she yelled at the horses to go faster.

Then Millie saw the first buffalo wallow. It was huge and was the size of a small crater. Instead of going around, she plowed right into it, the edge sending them in a skyward motion and landing with a hefty crack. Jim was sure the wagon was going to be torn apart and him with it. He bellowed at her to stop. Then they hit the other side of the wallow with disastrous results. Both Jim and Millie heard the splintering of the wagon when it hit the ground. Jim, by this time in tears of fright, looked behind him and saw a large crack emerging in the back of the buckboard.

"We're going to die!" he yelled at Millie.

Millie didn't return the shout; she just kept driving. The horses were beginning to tire, but Millie didn't seem to care. She had one purpose, and that was to get Jim to town before the people realized that there was no Jim Raymond on board the train. She screamed at the horses and was determined to get him home first.

After tufts, gopher holes, and another buffalo wallow, Millie sighted the town. She was coming in on the opposite side of town from the depot and pulled around the backside of the jail. She had no worries about Jim trying to escape when she transferred him to the prison. He was in such a state of shock that he followed her like a baby, went willingly into the cell, sat down, and simply stared, shaking.

Millie heard the train pull in and shouting coming from the depot. It was time for Ben to take over, and she went out to take care of the exhausted horses.

Ben came in all right, but not without a mob following him to the door yelling at him to bring Jim out. Ben paid no attention to their shouts and went into the cell to check in on the prisoner who still had a haunted look.

When Jim saw Ben, he started to cry. "Please," he begged, "please don't ever put me through that again. Hang me, shoot me, but never again put me in a buckboard with that crazy lady."

Jim got his wish.

It was high summer, and the judge decided to hold court outside under The Tree. It was a civilized trial except for a couple of onlookers yelling for Jim's skin. In the end, he was found guilty of horse theft, cattle rustling, and murder. They hanged him from a sturdy branch of The Tree.

1882: THE GAME

It began sprinkling just as Winnie was going out the door. *Well,* she thought, *that takes care of practice today.* But she went out anyway because she had to go to Colbert's, the larger general store in town. She picked out the colors of thread that she thought would be perfect for the curtains she was embroidering.

However, Winnie had a secret. She was disappointed there was going to be no baseball practice today as she loved the game. She had secretly begun hitting stones with a large branch that had fallen off an elm tree, but she had to do it in the woods near her home so no one could see her. Women were not allowed to play baseball. It wasn't proper. But after practicing with the stick and stones, she was sure she could hit a ball out of the park. The next best thing she could do was to go to the games in the park with The Tree and enjoy watching even though she thought she was better than half the players for the hometown Kings.

Practice was not called off. After the brief sprinkle, it cleared up and became sunny, and the grass became a bright, inviting green. So by two o'clock, the players on the Kings appeared for practice. Saturday would be the game against the Jacks, which was short for Jackrabbits, and the town was very excited. It had been a fierce rivalry all season long, but even the neighboring team, the Sailors, that had taken everything last season, couldn't keep up this year.

Donald Wayland had been her favorite player until he broke a bone in his foot and was unable to run like he used to. Now he was the umpire. That was the only thing that was ruining the season. Half the people in town didn't think he should be an umpire as he couldn't be impartial. The other half did. And there was a bit of an upset whenever he said, "Play ball!" Some fans booed, and some cheered.

It wasn't any secret in anybody's mind that Winnie was in love with Donald. She wanted to cheer for him when the game started, but, in the back of her mind, she thought maybe he was biased even though he assured everyone he wasn't.

Winnie's parents thought Donald should be thrown out, and they should get an umpire from the nearby town, the one that was too small to have a team of their own. That would be fair! But when they asked several candidates, they all wanted to know how much it paid. That was the end of that. But it didn't change her parents' minds. Of course, this left Winnie caught in the middle.

Donald and Winnie would go out at night, sometimes just to sit in the branch of The Tree that some unknown person had straightened decades ago and now made a good bench. However, sitting there made him a target for someone coming by to argue with him about a play he had called wrong.

"Why doesn't someone say I made a good call once in a while?" Donald mourned. "I do make them! But does anyone come by and slap me on the back and say, 'Good one, Donald!' No, they just want to pick at me."

"Then," Winnie countered, "just imagine he's saying, 'Good job, Donald!' happening every time someone berates your call. I have faith in you that you are trying your best to be unprejudiced in your decisions." She may have said that, but she only half meant it. "It's amazing," she continued, "that you can make those calls at all. They're split-second, and you have to call it as you see it. It must be very difficult." Now that she really meant.

Baseball practice that day was full of fans, and the small stands that were built for just a few were overrun. Mayor Childes made a notation that he should bring up new stands for the park at the next council meeting.

As usual, before Donald said, "Play ball!" he had to remind players of the town rule that was strictly enforced. "If The Tree is hit by a ball, batted, or thrown, that half of the inning is immediately over. And if The Tree is damaged in any way, the game is instantly over. Anyone caught trying to hurt The Tree for any reason will be thrown from the league. Okay, let's play ball!"

The park was large enough to play a good game of baseball without coming near the tree. However, the people of the town were so attached to The Tree; none of them could bear having any harm come to it. So the consequences were announced at every practice and regular game. Visiting teams seemed to understand and abide by the rules. The Tree had never been touched.

As far as Winnie was concerned, Donald made all the right calls that day, but not according to her parents and the other half of the town. Winnie decided that she was with Donald 100 percent. His judgments were quick and flawless. However, her father ranted against Donald all the way home.

"And you, Winnie," he said pointing right at her nose, "how can you keep company with a man like that? He has no idea what he was doing!"

"It was just a practice game, Father," she countered. "I think every call he made was right and quick. I saw nothing wrong with anything."

"Aw," her father growled, "what do you know? You're just a girl."

At that, Winnie stopped walking, turned around, and started back to the ballfield.

"Winnie!" her mother called, "Where are you going?"

"I'm going to find Donald. I'll be home for supper."

"I don't want you to have anything to do with that boy, Winnie," her father shouted after her.

Why don't you let everyone in town hear you, Dad? she sarcastically thought. By now, half the town was aware of his directive. But she kept walking toward the ball field.

She found Donald talking with several of the other Kings players. They seemed to be having a huddle, so she sat on the bleachers to wait. It wasn't long.

"I hear your dad doesn't want us to see each other anymore."

Winnie wasn't quite ready to know even Donald heard her father. It felt like a line drive to her chest. Recovering, she said, "I'm sorry you heard that, Donald."

"What are we going to do? I can't stop seeing you now. I think I'm in love with you. We can't let your father stop us just because he doesn't like some of the calls I make. You know how hard I try to be fair. We've talked about it."

"We can't let him call us out before we even come up to bat," she agreed. "But I don't know exactly what to do. You and the town obviously heard my father, and I will be watched by everyone. But I have an idea. You know that grove of trees by the river just downstream from the mill? You know the one. They all look like they were planted in a circle?"

"Oh, yeah. What about them?"

"That's my place to get away, and I spend a lot of time there. Meet me there tomorrow afternoon and bring a bat and a ball."

"Bring a what?" he asked incredulously.

"Just do it. Now I have to get home to help with supper. Tomorrow about four o'clock."

Winnie's father pumped her for information: Did she go see him? Did she tell him she can't see him anymore? She simply answered that she had to go see him to tell him what her father said even though he had heard him. Her father averted his eyes and cleared his throat several times.

"So what are you going to do?" he asked.

"Father, I'm in love with him. What can I do? It could mean I'm going to be an old maid and live with you and Mother forever if you don't watch out."

"But there are other young men. What about Eddie Watson at the dairy? He's always had eyes for you."

"I don't like Eddie. I never have."

"Well, my directive still stands. Donald is out!"

That night, after Winnie was in bed, she couldn't help thinking of what she was about to do. She was going to defy her father. Before Donald, that was a foul ball, but she was twenty-two now, and most of her friends were married. She was…"

Tap, tap, tap.

Winnie thought she was just imagining it. But there it was again, that tapping. She got out of bed, gathered her nightgown tightly around her, and raised the shade. She saw something leaning against the window, and then she saw Donald attached to the windowsill. She was so startled that she backed away and almost fell over her chair.

"What, in the name of Abner Doubleday, are you doing here?" she hoarsely whispered once she had recovered from the surprise.

"I just wanted to see you."

"I'm in my nightgown, for heaven's sake. Go away before my father catches you here."

"Haven't you been thinking about us?"

"It's only natural. I just don't want us to get caught."

"I just didn't want to drop the ball. I wanted you to know how much you mean to me."

"Good night, sweet prince. Steal home before you're caught missing."

She blew him a kiss, and he disappeared down the ladder.

The next afternoon, after telling her mother she was going to be out for a while, which was no lie, she walked about half a mile before she ended up in her grove of trees. Donald was there already. He grabbed his bat and ball, and she took his arm and walked to the far end of the grove. She relieved him of the equipment and directed him to the other side. With that, she tossed the ball up in the air, and *wham*! she hit line drive right to him. His face showed his amazement. Donald threw the ball back, and this time, it was a high pop-up. This time, he returned the ball with his best throw. She caught it without a glove. Then she let caution to the wind and hit a home run. Donald showed nothing but awe and a touch of jealousy.

"What do you think?" Winnie asked.

"When did you learn to do this?"

"I've been hitting stones with a tree branch for years. I've always wanted to try it with a real ball and bat."

"I wish you were able to play for the Kings. We'd slide into home every time."

"Well, I'm a girl, and I can't. But this was surely fun. I'll see you Saturday for the final game. I'm sure you will round all the bases with your decisions. I have to go." She squeezed his hand and trotted out of the grove.

Saturday was warm with a bright blue sky, and the Jacks arrived early to get in some batting practice. Winnie came early also so she could get a seat and watch Donald. The Kings politely waited their turn to practice. Winnie came to the conclusion that she really didn't care which team won; she just wanted to show her parents what a fair umpire Donald was. She had even talked to them at length about how he felt about baseball, that cheating just cheapened the sport he loved, and worked very hard to be fair. She hoped they listened.

The game started smoothly, and the score was even in the top of the third inning. The Jacks were up to bat, and the player hit a high pop-up. The sun was in Winnie's eyes, and she couldn't see where it went, but she found out quickly enough. It landed on her head.

The next thing she knew she had a splitting headache, and Doc Bailey's face was over her.

"How are you doing, Winnie?" he asked.

Winnie couldn't answer. All she could do was wish the entire Kings team would stop playing a game on her head.

"I have something that might help the pain. It's something new called aspirin. It's made from the boiled bark of the willow tree that people have been using for centuries against pain. Here you go. The pill and a glass of water. Drink it down."

Winnie tried, but she had no idea how to swallow a pill. Doc Bailey got another one, crushed it up, covered it with honey, and assured her she could get this one down. She could, but the taste of the pill kept coming through, and it was nasty.

The pill really didn't help much, and then she noticed her parents were there. And behind them was Donald. When she looked up at him, he put his finger to his lips. Apparently, her parents didn't know he was there.

But if he was there, who was umping the game between the Kings and the Jacks?

She found out in due time. The Jacks' umpire took over. The doctor's office wasn't far from The Tree park, and she could hear loud booing coming from the King's side of the stands. Apparently, their umpire was not doing his job for the Kings, and the townsfolk were about to riot. Winnie could hear various voices asking for "Donald, Donald, Donald!" Donald waved a small goodbye to her and left the doctor's office and went back to the game. She could hear a cheer when he made his appearance.

"Where was that boy all this time?" her father asked.

"Why would he leave the game?" her mother inquired.

Winnie croaked out. "He was here, right behind you, to see if I was going to be all right."

Her parents didn't say a word.

When the pain stopped raging and had become more blunt than sharp, and she could walk steadily, she went and sat under The Tree. The park was now empty. The game was over, and the Kings lost by a large margin. Donald came and sat beside her followed by her parents who appeared to be contrite.

The game and the score soon became history, but Donald emerged as a hero. Half the town was eating crow while the other half could have said, "I told you so," but didn't.

Two years later, Winnie married Jonas Hart, an old classmate who returned from a stint in the Navy, and their friendship caught fire. And Donald? He's still umping, still looking for that love of his life. He and Winnie remain friends.

1897: THE HYMNAL

Elsa was almost trembling. She was going to buy her first book in English. She may have been born in Jönköping, Sweden, but now she was an American, having immigrated in 1897, making her way to Nebraska. She knew she needed to be fluent. The people she worked for as a maid, the Mayfields, were so kind to her and patient with her poor attempts at communication that she had decided to surround herself with English. Among other things, it meant she would go to the local church to attend services in her adopted language.

She picked up the book she wanted. It was leather, the brand-new version of the hymnal, which she opened carefully. There were the words in English that gave her so much comfort in Swedish, and she wondered if it would ever feel the same.

She walked, looking for a place to sit and really look at her treasure, until she came to the old oak tree way off the side of the road. It was more than huge. It looked as if it wanted to pick her up and put her under its leafy canopy. So at The Tree's bidding, she sat down and began to read her book. After a while, she closed the book and leaned it against The Tree's trunk. She felt a tremendous amount of joy and comfort. This was going to be her place.

Oskar Lindskoog, Elsa's husband, was stubborn and refused to even consider learning English in that way, but he had no objection to Elsa exposing their two children, Hannah and Viktor, to the English-speaking church. And so they went, minus Oskar, to the English services. The only Swedish the children heard was when their parents slipped mistakenly into their native language. Gradually, even that was lost.

Contemplating this change wasn't easy, but all it took was a trip to The Tree. An extra hour of thought and conjecture under The Tree made her language transition easier. That is until she realized that her thoughts were in Swedish. *But*, she thought, *The Tree didn't mind.*

In early 1925, Hannah Lindskoog Mayfield, Elsa and Oskar's daughter, was in church, the same one she and her husband had grown up in, when it was announced that coming soon were new hymnals. The pastor said that the old hymnals had served their purpose, but the new ones would make the Swedish and English churches into one. Elsa smiled and nudged her daughter: She had done that years ago.

When the new hymnals arrived, Hannah was happy to see that the regal *thee* and *thou* were still there. In spite of many things being changed, she enthusiastically embraced the new. Her mother clung to the old. She shared her feelings with The Tree and was rewarded with satisfaction and a sense of peace, just as her mother did.

It wasn't until 1958 when Hannah was in her sixties that she heard a new hymnal was coming with a new order of service. That meant possibly a chunk of her cozy world could fall by the wayside. The service was so ingrained in her psyche that she would often hum the liturgy around the house. Her son, Thomas, born in 1922, was thirty-six and had his own family. Hannah's husband and her mother, Elsa, had both died in 1950. Thomas and his brood moved into the very mansion he grew up in and his grandmother had worked as a maid. Hannah had married the owner's son. Now, Hannah reveled in her own area of the house near the kitchen, and she enjoyed even more having total access to her grandchildren. And, like it or not, those children went to church and Sunday school with her. It was mostly not liked. "Church is boring! Sunday school is dumb!" they complained. Too bad. They were going. All Thomas ever said to them was, "I went, you will too." Thomas went to church once in a while, but it was mostly Hannah who took them with their feet digging into the carpet to make it as hard as possible for Mormor to drag them.

It turned out that Hannah was totally right. She hated the new liturgy. It was far away from anything of comfort to her. All familiarity seemed to have been flung out the door with no regard for her. She sulked, and even her grandson, Greg, who was the most sympathetic boy she had ever known, was no help. Now she knew how her mother had felt, hanging on to that little hymnal she bought at the turn of the century. Strangely, the children actually liked the new order of service. "Church is boring" was replaced with, "I like the new songs, Mormor. Don't you? And best of all, the book is red! That's my favorite color."

Maybe, she thought, *maybe I should give it a chance.* So she made a trip to The Tree for contemplation and a chance to renew, just as her mother used to do.

Hannah was in for another change. It was 1978, and she was not living where she wanted to be: She was in a nursing home. Thomas and Greg both told her they just could not keep up with her needs, in spite of the protests of Linda, Thomas' wife, that she could do it. Linda had to admit she wasn't a spring chicken any longer, but she loved Mormor, and it was even more difficult to see her in a home that it was for Hannah herself to be there.

One day, Michael, Greg's middle child, came in with a wrapped package for her. Under the wrapping was a brand-new liturgy book. Michael told her this was the latest, and she could follow the service on the radio since the church broadcast every Sunday. Hannah gave her great-grandson a hug for his thoughtfulness. She glumly thumbed through it. She had finally gotten used to the red book, and now they're forcing a green one on her? Bah! And her beloved *thees* and *thous* were gone for good. But what could she do?

Michael stood by her, beaming and telling her it was really cool! She smiled at him and checked out the book again. Look at all the new hymns! She thought, *Now I'll have something to try out on the piano in the rec room.*

Hannah was called home in 1980 at the age of eighty-five. Thomas and Linda, now empty nesters, decided to move out of the mansion and into something smaller and where the weather was warmer. That meant taking on the chore of cleaning out the basement and the attic so the house would be saleable. Greg was happy living where he was but really didn't want anything so pretentious, so the old mansion that had been in the family since the turn of the century would be sold. Cleaning out the house was a backbreaking chore, but Thomas and Linda, and occasionally Greg and his wife, Susan, would help out. Going through an exceptionally dusty box, Susan remarked, "Look at this, will you! It has to be a hundred years old!" The others gathered around and looked at the small volume she held. Thomas brightened and gently took the little book from her.

"This belonged to my grandmother, Elsa. She's the one who came over from Sweden. I remember her taking this to church with her every week even when it was out of date. She held onto that hymnal like it was a talisman."

Greg took the book from his father's hands. "Look at this liturgy, will you? I'm glad we don't have to go through that gobbledygook. They have the pastor going on and on! Look, it lists the hymns, but there's no music. How did that work? And the only thing I recognize in here is the place marked *sermon*. Geeze! All these *thee*s and *thou*s. It sounds more Quaker than anything."

"What shall we do with it?" Linda asked. She turned it over, and some papers fell out of it. "Oh, gee, I hope that's not pages that are coming out."

"No," Thomas said, retrieving it. "It's a newspaper clipping. It's an obit. It's Elsa's. Mormor must have put it in there. Look, it even gives the date she came from Sweden, the town she lived in there, and her parents' names. You know, I'll bet we have family there. I wonder if we should contact them."

Elsa's little English hymnal was put away carefully in a place where they would remember. And surprisingly, they did remember. In 2006, the church produced yet another version of the hymnal; and this time, the whole family went to church: Michael and his bride, Lindsay; Greg and Linda, now in their sixties; and Thomas, now in his eighties and widowed just a year. They brought Elsa's little hymnal along so it could be in church again. The "cranberry" hymnal, as it was called, wasn't much different from the green, but it offered a greater variety of music and settings. Lindsay thought the changes were great. She said keeping up with what the people would relate to was very important. Greg, however, had something to say about tradition. It needs to be kept!

"You agree with me, don't you, Mike?" Lindsay asked. "Don't you hope that the church keeps on making changes and going with the flow?"

"Lindsay," Greg countered, "keeping tradition is rather like a cup of coffee on a cold day. It's warm, familiar, and comforting. Michael, don't you hope we keep our roots deep and intact?"

Michael looked at his wife and his father. "I hope so. I certainly hope so." And he thought of The Tree, sitting under it, with its deep roots, and he smiled.

1922: THE CAMPAIGN

It was an amazing day for the town: Flags were flying on every house, church bells pealed, and the people gathered in The Tree's town square park to hear the mayor speak. Today was the day that their town would be declared the county seat.

It had been a long tussle with the neighboring town for the honor of becoming the seat, and tussle was a mild verb. There had been fights of all kinds and even one person shot, all in the name of the county seat. This was because many years ago, before the turn of the century, a surveyor had dropped a lens cap while determining the town lines. He never found the cap, but everyone figured that the one person who would find the cap could declare the winner of the county seat.

A shy and very solitary man, Marcus Calhoun, had found it on his back forty, ten, maybe fifteen years earlier. He was doing the spring plowing when he saw a flash of metal and stopped the horses to investigate. He didn't know what it was because he was living a self-chosen, cloistered lifestyle and hadn't even heard of the feud between the two towns, or what he dug up would mean. Marcus thought the metal cap might amuse his cat, so he stuck it in his pocket and forgot about it. Much later, when Marcus was old and too infirmed to take care of himself, his grandson was helping him move into town where he would live with his daughter and her family, the grandson found the lens cap.

"Gramps, where did you get this?" Jim asked.

"That? Oh, I think I found that one day while I was plowing. I thought it might be fun for Cranky."

"Do you have any idea where exactly you found it?"

"Jimmy, given enough time I could remember anything."

"Think, Gramps, think. This could mean a whole lot to the town."

"What? That little piece of metal? I only kept it because Cranky liked it so much. Now that he's gone, I have something to remember him by."

Impatiently, Jim pleaded, "What field were you plowing that day?

"Let's see," Marcus answered scratching his chin, "I think it was the back forty. Yeah, I'm sure that was the one 'cause I was thinking that this was the last field, and I was tired."

"Do you remember exactly where in the back forty?"

"Aw, c'mon, young 'un! I was lucky to remember which field it was."

"But," said Jim getting more and more excited, "it was the back forty? The closest one to County Line Road?"

"Yup, that's about right. Why is that so important?"

Jim related the story of the lens cap.

"So that proves that our town is now the county seat!"

"Well," Marcus said looking at the old cap, "isn't that something. And here I thought it was a cat toy."

The town was grateful to Marcus and wanted him to give a speech under The Tree with Mayor Timmons. But true to his ways, Marcus never showed up.

The town carried on with the mayor's rhetoric that left most of the people speechless. Mayor Timmons announced that The Tree would be cut down, and a beautiful new courthouse would be built on the site. Bulldozers and other equipment would be there in the morning to start the job.

The people began talking among themselves, some shouting at the mayor.

"You can't cut down The Tree!"

"The Tree is the heart and soul of this town."

"How dare you even entertain such a murder."

Finally, Mayor Timmons was able again to catch their attention.

"I would never be so callous as to cut down The Tree and toss it for the sake of a building," he orated. "The oak wood from this tree will be used in supporting and decorating the county seat building. Now what's wrong with that?"

Even the mayor's wife, who had been left out of the mayor's plans, got up on the stage and said, "You do that, and I'll make myself a widow!"

The mayor shut up for a change.

The sheriff got up on the stage with the mayor and his wife and signaled for quiet.

"Friends," Sheriff Blanton said in his folksy way, "let's not jump all over each other. We had enough of that when we were fighting about which town would be the county seat. After all, we live in a democratic society. We can vote on it. We can do that, can't we, Mayor?"

The mayor, articulation still failing him, nodded.

"Okay, Mayor Timmons, when can we have this election?" said someone from the crowd.

Getting his voice back, the mayor took a piece of paper out of his pocket. He cleared his throat twice. "Important elections always seem to be held on Tuesdays, so why don't we make it the twenty-first? That would give both sides of the issue time to campaign." Then, in a smaller voice said, "And I'll cancel the bulldozers. For now."

The crowd broke up with considerable vocalizations with one another.

"Our precious Tree turned into firewood?"

"Look at it this way: When we cut it down, we'll be able to count the rings and know for sure how old it was."

"Don't talk about The Tree as if it were already gone. There are too many people against cutting it down."

"But we really need a courthouse that would bring more order to the place."

"I agree we need a courthouse, but not at The Tree's expense."

"Why does it have to be where The Tree is? There's plenty of land around town."

"The town doesn't have that kind of money."

"Hey, come on! It's just a tree," a man finally said.

For his effort, he was smacked in the mouth by a purse-wielding matron.

So the campaign went. People argued on the street, put signs outside their houses, even carried signs with them when they went to town. It seemed to be a fifty-fifty battle.

Within a few days, the leaders of each group were defined. Alvin Hersch, a dry goods merchant whose store looked out over the square, became the pro-Tree leader while Parker Lawson, who owned a bar and grill, became the opposition leader. Alvin soon became concerned that one of Parker's group would try to cut down or damage the tree in the middle of the night. He arranged a schedule of guards. At one point, the first Girl Scout troop in the area came to rescue The Tree by spending the night camping out in the square. Parker was dead set against losing the county seat to a damned tree. People were constantly in the square campaigning for or against The Tree. Divisions were defined, and there was no neutral ground.

Marcus Calhoun saw all this from his room at his daughter's house that was a block from the square. He just shook his head at the brouhaha for which he felt responsible. What a harebrained bunch of people lived in the town! No wonder he had preferred a solitary life once his wife had died.

Three days before the election, things got personal and intense. Parker's group insinuated that Alvin's dry goods store vastly overcharged people because his was the only one in the town. Alvin's faction boldly accused Parker of running a prostitution ring in his saloon. On hearing this, Marcus was sickened. Neither assembly was correct, and both needed to shut up. The election was very close, and they would have to live with these accusations for many years. Marcus didn't want to have such divisions live on.

Being high summer, the weather was quirky, freaky, and sometimes downright terrorizing. But these hearty folks had been through it before and would be through it again. From his window, however, Marcus could see something stirring in the clouds, and the air felt, as he put it, *electric*. He couldn't think of any other way to get it across. And to him, it meant a rough bout with the winds and rain. He was glad he was sheltered by the town and not alone in his farm out on the open prairie.

By midday, the worst of the worst clouds had gathered, spitting lightning and pelting rain. The prairie sky turned an ominous purple. From his window, Marcus could see people charging for the nearest doorway for shelter. It hit, as most tornados do, with the sound like a rushing, roaring train. Violent winds sucked the breath out of the town, and the sound of explosions could be heard over the raw tempest.

In spite of being hit head-on, the town was still full of life in the same compliment. Yes, there were people who were hurt, a few badly, but there were plenty of people on hand to help dig them out of the rubble. One lady had a door fall on her breaking her arm and leg, while another was caught under the roof of a house that was separated from its structure when the wind grabbed it by the eaves. The explosions were from houses that had all their window closed by their residents trying to protect themselves from the storm, but pressure built up, and the buildings couldn't take it. One family that had taken shelter in their basement found there was no upstairs when the storm abated.

Marcus congratulated himself and his family for not closing windows and going for shelter in the basement with the dirt floor. Not one speck of dust was disturbed.

When it was over and people began to come out, they looked around. Most of the town was still intact with the exception of the few that had blown up. Marcus and his family also came out. Marcus's daughter, Linda, was a registered nurse, so she grabbed her bag and went out in search of those who needed her.

From where he stood, Marcus could see the whole path of the storm. It ran through the middle of everything, even through the park where The Tree was. He only hoped that The Tree was still living. He finally saw it, alive and green, well, most of it. The tornado had stripped off leaves from a few large branches, and Marcus had to see what condition it was in. He began to walk over to the park. It wasn't easy since there were boards thrown around everywhere, and a car that had been picked up and landed on its top was in the middle of First Street.

Once at The Tree, he was convinced it was still sound. But what he didn't see was his house. Not his daughter's house, but the house his wife owned and lived in before they were married. She had abandoned the house the day they got married to live in his prairie farmhouse. When she died twenty years later, he got possession of it. Marcus didn't have to walk a step as the house was the only house, or what was left of it, on the west side of the town square.

"Dad!" Marcus could hear Linda's voice, half scolding, half frustrated. "What in the world are you doing out in this rubble field? I'm going to get Jim to help you get back home. We're one of the lucky ones to have a house and no one hurt. You wait right here for Jim."

Marcus supposed she was right; however, it occurred to him that no one in his family even knew he owned property in town, much less on the town square. He decided to keep it to himself a bit longer.

The cleanup continued for the next two days with men and women working doggedly to clear paths, streets, and what was left of houses. Neighboring towns came to help with cleanup, first aid, and to bring supplies like water. Marcus noticed that people from Alvin's pro-side of The Tree and Parker's con-side were working together to save their town.

The election was upon them, but there were no ballots, no ballot boxes, and no place to vote. A gathering began to take place under The Tree with people asking questions. Finally, the mayor came in to calm the crown down.

"Folks, we don't have the facilities for an election."

"But we need the answer now," someone shouted.

"How about we get this over with by a hand vote? I've had enough of this campaigning stuff."

"We have other works more important," another answered.

"Now that's a good idea," the mayor said approvingly. "Does anyone object?"

There was a unity of shaking heads and murmurs of "no."

"Okay, then, if you're ready, it's time to vote."

More nodding.

"All those in favor of cutting down The Tree to make way for a courthouse and use its wood to furnish the courthouse, raise your hand."

Hands went up. Several men counted the hands, and when they were satisfied they had the correct number, the mayor asked for hands that The Tree be spared. The same people counted and agreed on a number.

The mayor looked at the tallies and said, "We have a dead tie here. And that is not acceptable. We need to vote again."

They voted again, again, and again. It all came out the same: a tie.

After the last vote, Marcus, who never told Linda he was going to the square, spoke up. The sound of a strange voice focused everyone's attention on the recluse.

"Now, I know that I don't mess with most people. I enjoy my solitude too much, but there is something I need to say. You all see what destruction that storm brought. And, if you had taken time away from that stupid campaigning, you would see that it made us a town again, one group working in harmony with another group. The campaign forgotten. And I'm here to tell you that no one needs to get in his neighbor's hair over this again. If you can see that the house over on the west side of the square was destroyed. I own that house and that land, and I think it would be a peachy place to build a courthouse. It takes the whole west, so a new courthouse can be built there, and The Tree will stand. We just have to expand the square with the park in the middle and the courthouse on the side. And, as of now, I am donating that land to the town for the county seat. That is providing all you people quit this fersnookin bickering and be neighbors again."

The crowd was dead silent for about three seconds, then a huge roar of approval ripped through the town.

Marcus took that moment to slip out. The last thing he wanted was to have people slapping him on the back or, worse, women kissing his cheek.

Back in his room at Linda's house, he settled into his favorite chair, picked up a book, and turned the outside world off. He was proud of what he had done, and it was right. After all, that piece of metal he found in the cornfield that his cat, Cranky, liked so much had started all that. He had ended it. And he had gotten rid of that useless piece of land.

Marcus was seen once in a while in town, but he kept mostly to himself as he liked it. When the town council tried to talk him into letting them name the building the Marcus Calhoun building, he had one word to say.

"Piffelfarf!"

1932: THE TIN LIZZY

There was nothing unusual or outstanding about Dreyfuss Underwood. His first name, maybe, but that was a family name and his mother always emphasized he needed to be proud of it. He wasn't particularly, but he put up with it. The name didn't lend itself to a nickname, so he was simply called "Dreyfuss."

But there were always nicknames that were of the unkind nature. He knew a boy at school whose name was Gower Kieser, Gower being a family name also. He was known throughout the school as "Flower Kisser." But that was the one thing that made Dreyfuss outstanding. His nicknames were worse than poor Gower's. He was known as "Dry Underwear" or "Fussy Underpants." And since it was mainly Johnny McMurray who led the campaign to put Dreyfuss down, there was nothing unusual about that name that lent itself to any kind of imitation, so Dreyfuss just tried to ignore the taunts.

Dreyfuss thought Johnny would stop with the name-calling once he grew up a bit, but it only increased. By seventh grade, it was constant and interfered with his studies.

Since it was the Depression, Dreyfuss was actually lucky to be in school at all. A lot of the other boys were taken out by their parents and made to help out on the farm, the store, or anywhere they were needed. Although their farm was heavily mortgaged, his parents realized the importance of education and insisted he stay in school. Dreyfuss wasn't so sure he wanted to stay in school with the constant bombardment of nasty names he was getting from Johnny as well as from the few other boys that were left.

Eventually, Johnny graduated and went on to high school while things at the Underwood home got dire, and Dreyfuss had to quit school to help his father. This was perfectly all right with him since he didn't have any friends there, and Johnny and company had made school almost a horrific experience for him. He didn't have any interaction with Johnny any longer, but he had heard there was a new target at school. Dreyfuss remembered Dusty Heinman ("Dusty Hymie") in his prayers.

About 1935, the farm was recovering; and, as Dreyfuss would put it, "They were eating regular." As the result of the hard work and deprivation, he was never as tall as his father; and, as his mother said, "He was so thin you could see right through him." But he was strong, and fueled with his mother's good cooking, he managed to keep the farm going after his father died. Dreyfuss's mother was called home a year later.

All that was left was the farm and an old Tin Lizzy. The car became an interest, and Dreyfuss spent hours tinkering with it. He replaced, tightened, put into place, and oiled until it sputtered into life. And that's all it did, sputter. It wouldn't go anywhere. That was the knot he wasn't sure how to untie, so he went to Doc's Garage in town, towing the Lizzy with his horse and wagon.

Walking into the office of the garage, his blood iced up as he heard, "Hey, there, Fussy Underpants!" He could feel his face redden in rage and humiliation at the sound of Johnny's voice.

"Don't call me that, Johnny," he said as calmly as he could and without even turning around.

"Whaz a matter, Fussy? Aren't you glad to see me after all these years?"

Not knowing where to go from there, he remained silent. He knew Johnny would take just about anything he said and turn it against him. He didn't want to go through seventh grade all over again.

"So what did you bring Doc to fix today? Have you actually gotten yourself a car? I can't imagine you driving a car. I'm going to look at it."

Johnny went out the door and a minute later came back laughing. "You call *that* a car?"

Yes, the Tin Lizzy was old, but she had very little rust left on her, and she sort of ran, and he was proud of the way he had taken her out of the back of the barn and fixed her up the way she was when he was little and his dad would let him *help* drive as they rode to town. And she was all his!

With a change of voice tone, Johnny asked, "Would you sell it to me?"

Without thinking, Dreyfuss said with a calm but decisive "No!"

"Okay, Mr. Underpants. Just asking. Who'd want a hunk of junk like that anyway?"

Dreyfuss bit his tongue. No more fuel for Johnny's fire. He turned and went into the garage to find Doc. They spoke for a few minutes then Doc went to give the Lizzy a once-over.

"Your drive train is stuck," Doc came up with. "Won't take but a minute to loosen it up, and then she should run like a Lizzy should." Doc was as good as his word.

Dreyfuss hooked the Lizzy up to his wagon and towed it back to his farm. Driving onto his land and looking at his burgeoning fields made him proud, just as the Lizzy did. His parents would have been gratified by Dreyfuss's achievements.

Over the next year, he heard some disquieting things from town. It was Johnny said this and Johnny said that about Dreyfuss. All were untrue and some quite scandalous. But he was powerless to stop the talk.

While in Happ's Grocery Store one rainy morning, Dreyfuss saw two women he knew who had been friends of his mother. They were deep in conversation, heads bent together, quite oblivious of their surroundings until one of them glanced up and saw Dreyfuss. She quickly nudged her friend and pointed at Dreyfuss. They both stopped talking and went on their ways. He knew it was about him, so he went after the shorter of the two women.

"Celia," he called after her. She stopped, and he caught up with her. "I haven't seen you in such a long time! How are you?"

She looked nervously at him. "Well," she stammered, "you know. I'm fine. Edgar has the arthritis. The store is doing well again."

"What's wrong? You sound nervous," Dreyfuss asked, trying to get some information out of her.

"Oh, no, not nervous at all. Why would you say that?"

"You and Millie were in such deep conversation that you were surprised to see me, and then you quit talking. It was me you were talking about, wasn't it, Celia?"

"Well, you know. About that girl that came to your house looking for food, how you took her in and all. Oh, I'm sorry I'm such a gossip, but we're all wondering when you're going to marry her?"

"There's no girl. I live alone. Where did you hear that piece of news?"

"Well, it's all over town, just like that thing about the fishing trip you took, and you almost drowned your friend."

"There was no fishing trip and no friend. Again, where did you get that gossip from?"

I heard it from Winifred Mayer who heard it from Clara Stokes, and I think she heard it from Doc."

"And Doc heard it from Johnny McMurray, I'll bet."

Celia nodded. "Could be. Johnny does like to talk."

"And not a word he says is true. Thank you, Celia, for your honesty."

Dreyfuss left the store hoping to make it the three blocks back to where he parked the Lizzy, but the rain was too hard, so he ran across the street to the park where The Tree was growing. He ducked under the sheltering leaves. Noting that the ground was a bit muddy and the benches were soaked, he leaned against The Tree in a standing position.

There was no way to stop Johnny. He knew from past experience that he would never be able to persuade him to stop spreading lies, and he wasn't about to counter with lies. He stood for a while, blankly thinking.

It was as if The Tree infused him with an idea so radical that it even surprised him. But did he dare to do it? It wasn't illegal or morally wrong; it was just a whole different approach. And it was the only thing that would stop the lies being heaped upon him.

Dreyfuss turned to the tree, patted it twice, and said in a whisper, "Thanks, old friend." And he ran down the road to the Lizzy, feeling so light and joyful he didn't even realize he was getting soaked.

When he got home, he shined up the Tin Lizzy to its brightest, painted what was chipped, and cleaned the neglected top.

A few days later when things had dried up, he hitched the Lizzy to the horse and wagon and drove into town. He found Johnny McMurray's house, halted the horse, and got out of the wagon. Remembering his time under The Tree, he took a deep breath and knocked on Johnny's door.

"What do you want?" was Johnny's greeting.

"You see that car?" Dreyfuss asked pointing at the Lizzy.

"Yeah. What about it?"

"It's yours." Dreyfuss turned and walked away.

To the end of his days, Dreyfuss never heard another snip of unkind gossip about himself.

1943: THE RADIO

Joey chuckled to himself as he fastened the last wire into The Tree.

How could such and plain, ugly box require such elaborate dressings? And why had it been so hard to find? Yes, it was wartime, and most scrap metals had gone for the war effort, but he was able to find the short-wave radio in a dark corner of Otis' barn. Luckily Otis didn't charge him much for the thing, but it was exactly what Joey wanted.

The radio was something Joey had dreamed of, stuck as he was in the middle of Nebraska, aka nowhere. He dreamed of faraway places and people, but there was no going anywhere during the war. But at least with this radio, he could get news and ideas from all around the world, or as far as the signal would go. He was about to use it again, maybe this time with luck someone will answer.

When he got the radio, the antenna was broken off, and Otis didn't have a clue where it might be—not that it would do him any good anyway. So as much as he knew about radios, he jerry-rigged the antenna into six different wires that had to be up in the air. Joey didn't think The Tree would mind being a part of the antenna system.

Joey gave his call sign and asked if there was anyone out there. He asked several times, but he got nothing but air. Suddenly, a voice blasted from the radio confirming that the thing did work; and at the top of its voice, Joey turned down the volume and answered the call.

"Where are you?" Joey asked.

"In Oklahoma. And you?" the voice inquired.

"Nebraska. I used to live in Oklahoma."

"What's your name?" asked the voice.

"Joey. Joey Miller. And yours?"

"Stands Alone."

"You must be from the reservation," Joey came back.

"Yeah. How do you know about it?" Stands Alone said with surprise.

"My dad was the doctor there. He was born on the reservation."

"Where is he now?"

"He died about six years ago, and Mom wanted to move back to where she grew up. She a Pawnee. I'm half Pawnee and half Navajo."

"Do you speak Navajo or Pawnee?" asked Stands Alone, his voice growing more excited.

"I grew up on the Navajo reservation, so I learned that before I learned English. I speak some Pawnee, but most people around here speak English."

"Have you heard about the call for men who speak Navajo?"

"Why would anyone want Navajo speakers?" Joey asked, very confused.

"It's for the war. It had something to do with speaking in Navajo code on the radio so the enemy can't understand it."

"Are you going to be one of those?" Joey asked.

"No, I'm too old. I'm seventy-two, and that's way past what they're looking for."

"I'm almost old enough. I turn eighteen next month."

"You obviously like the radio, and you'll be of age soon. You might want to look into it." Stands Alone's voice was fading, and a crackling began coming between the two of them.

Then he was gone.

Joey spit out a few choice words in Navajo. Still, he had at last connected with someone on his radio! He tried several times to reconnect with Stands Alone with no luck. He'd try again tomorrow at the same time.

Joey and his mother now lived on family land in Clay County. Hastings was the nearest town with any number of people. Joey and his mom and dad had lived on the Navajo reservation in Oklahoma where he was born. By the time he was twelve, his father passed away from what Joey's mother called "overwork and overwrought." With very few doctors, he was almost never home; and when he did come home, he couldn't stop worrying about this case or that, supplies that didn't come, or even his own skills as a doctor.

When he got back home that night, he couldn't stop thinking about what Stands Alone said about a radio talker. He spoke fluent Navajo, and he could work a radio. So why not?

His mom was in the kitchen busy with dinner preparations when he went in to ask her.

"Mom, you know I have a birthday coming up next month."

"I remember the day well. I was there when it happened," she quipped.

"I want something really different for my birthday this year."

"And what could that be?"

Joey took a deep breath, let it out, and said, "I want your permission to join the Marines."

There was a dead silence. He saw his mother's head droop, and she sighed deeply.

"Well, Joey," she said lifting her head, "I was wondering when you were going to show an interest in going off to war. But why the Marines?"

"They're calling for Navajo speakers. It has something to do with speaking in the tongue so the Germans can't break the code. Mom, you know how much I love the radio, and I really want to see some of the world before I'm too old to appreciate it."

His mother stood straight and said, "Of course you may join the Marines."

"Then it's okay if I go over to the recruiting station in Hastings and find out more about the program? I still have to wait until next month to join."

"Go, Joey, and may God go with you."

The next morning, dressed in his Sunday suit, he went to the recruiting station, and he found out some realities. He would go to boot camp, then he would go to school to learn the code, but only after he proved he really could speak Navajo.

It was a long three weeks between the interview and his birthday, but the day he turned eighteen, he arrived in the recruiting office, ready and very willing.

The next few months were a blinding collage of boot camp, which he sort of enjoyed, and then code school. He was under such a veil of secrecy that he learned that if knowledge of the code was threatened, he would be shot so he couldn't spill secrets.

Joey's first language was Navajo, but he had learned it as any child learned a language. But in code school, he found out what a complex grammar system it was. The numerous dialects, the complex syntax, and phonology made it impossible for anyone to comprehend who had not had extensive exposure and training. Joey sailed through code school. It was a homecoming of a sort. However, learning the military way to use a short wave was an eye-opener. He thought of how he had used that old radio from Otis and had to laugh at his own ignorance.

He was deployed to many different places in the United States and then to England. Here he found the language almost unintelligible when spoken quickly! He found the London-style of the language was almost funny. But he learned to say "lorry" for truck, understanding that "ergotthechippanon" meant it was time for dinner, and it was ale they drank not beer.

In June of 1944, he was awakened in the middle of the night in a hushed manner and swept off to a transport. He wasn't told where he was going until the plane was airborne. He was then told he and other code talkers were going to Saipan. Joey had never heard of it. He thought that since it ended in "pan," it must be near to Japan. He was right.

Joey's usually sunny attitude faced overwhelming opposition once they landed. Saipan was a sea of mud, abandoned huts, and caves. There were remnants of a civilian population, but only the structures were left standing. He wondered where the people went.

The radios were set up outside in a cave so they were away from the rain. He was told they found a family hiding in that cave and had chased them out. He also heard that a large number of civilians had been killed due to close-quarter fighting. He wanted the fighting to be over so no more civilians would die. That would not prove possible.

The fighting lasted twenty-five days from June over to July. The battle was tumultuous, and the messages sent back and forth during that time were lightning fast and never-ending. Joey was busy every minute he was on duty, and he kept waiting for the message to say something about the end of the battle.

The end did come in early July, but the harm to the civilian population was frightening. He heard that more than one thousand civilians committed suicide by jumping off Banzai Cliff rather than being taken prisoners by the Americans. And that was only a part of some twenty thousand civilian deaths. Joey almost felt responsible for this: The more messages that got through with his help only seemed to boost the ghastly obliteration.

Two days after the end of the conflict, Joey was called to speak with "someone in charge," he was told. He had been so buried in his work, the mud, and the thought of the loss of civilians that he hadn't had any time to think about who might be in charge. With curiosity piqued, he reported to a half-blown-up house that served as a sort of headquarters.

"Miller?"

"Yes, Sir."

"You've done a good job. Took over shifts when others were too beat. Why did you do that?"

"I like the radio, sir."

"Interesting. By the way, if you're Navajo, what is your tribal name? And not in Navajo, I don't understand that. Tell me in English."

"My name means 'Pulverizer of Grain.'"

"Oh. Interesting. Is that why you have the last name of Miller?"

"Yes, Sir."

"Why the 'Joseph' part of it?"

"My mother liked it."

"Interesting. Well, Miller, you're in line for something a bit less stressful. I can't give you any R and R right now—you're needed badly everywhere. So I'm going to have you shipped to Hawaii. Nice place for work, and play is only a few steps away. That is if you can get away. You're in demand and doing a damn good job. I hope I run into you again some time."

"Thank you, Sir."

Hawaii was just as he imagined. He had talked to enough people in Hawaii in the Navajo code. He found that there was even time to relax and try to deal with the nightmarish situation on Saipan. There was nothing he could do about it. He knew that. But the phantasm still lingered.

While he was there, he became the representative for his division to discuss shortcomings with the code, add new terms into the system, and update their codebooks. Joey was sent to other code talkers to train others who could not attend the meeting. Things were looking up.

Then, in February of '45, he was sent to an island that was a major initiative of the Pacific Campaign. It was Iwo Jima, and it saw some of the fiercest fighting of the war. Major Connor of the Fifth Marine Division signal officer had six Navajo Code Talkers on duty at all times. The first two days of the battle, eight hundred messages were sent and received with no errors. Later, Major Connor was heard to say that the Battle of Iwo Jima was won by the Navajo Code Talkers.

Joey decided he couldn't afford to keep tally of casualties anymore.

The war ended soon after, and Joey was sent home. He had had half of his pay sent home to his mother, but she had saved it for him instead of using it for herself. It annoyed Joey, but since he arrived back in Nebraska dead broke, he was glad she hadn't used it for anything. He decided to save as much of it as he could and take her on a vacation.

Joey got the job back that he had before he was deployed, working as a sous-chef in a restaurant in Hastings. While trying not to chop off any fingers, his mind wandered back to Saipan and Iwo Jima. Try as he would, he couldn't get those places out of his mind. Finally, he decided that he never would accept the memories, good and bad.

But he missed his radio. He worked on the one he got from Otis and got it into working order, but he still had to attach the antennae leads to The Tree. It was okay for someone who didn't know much about radios, but he was a professional, and he wanted a new radio.

It was time to sell his old one, antennae leads and all.

Joey thought about how the radio had affected his life. And he thought of the next person to own it. How would that life be affected?

1955: THE PEN PAL

Miss. Payton was very excited about her new project for the class. As soon as possible, everyone had to have a pen pal. Sam was hardly enthusiastic, but it was a class assignment, and he had to have the name, location, and birthdate of the pen pal within one month. She didn't care if the pen pal was someone as far away as France or as close as someone across town, but it had to be some person where no acquaintance existed.

"This project," she said, "will sharpen your writing and social skills. We'll have each pen pal's birthday celebrated here, and your pen pal will receive something special from you. Now, are there any questions?"

"Does that mean we'll be having a party on each of their birthdays? Like cupcakes and cookies and stuff?" asked Tonya.

"No, dear, it will mean that that name will be on a special section of the board, so we'll all know their names, where they live, and who their pen pal in the class is. We will have another class project to get ideas what to send these people for their birthdays and how we will make and send them."

"What about people who have birthdays in the summer?" Tonya always asked the most questions.

"We'll send them their gifts before school is out for the summer."

"Where will we find these pen pals?"

"Good question, Tonya. I have a copy of an address for all of you to a service in New York called 'Pen Pals 4U,' and they will send you a form to fill out so they can match you with someone. You should have a name in a few weeks."

Grudgingly, Sam took the address when it was passed around. It cost two dollars for the service. He'd have to scrape together the money from his allowance.

With the form filled out, Sam mailed it in and promptly forgot about it. That is until the mailman brought the response. Sam opened the envelope gingerly.

"A girl! I can't write to a girl! I don't even like to talk to the girls in my class!" He looked over the form he filled out and saw that he hadn't checked his preference for a boy or girl. For a moment, he seriously thought of sending it back and asking for a change of gender, but then he remembered the two dollars. He was stuck with Sally Holtzer from California. Sam put his head down on the kitchen table and groaned.

Just then Sam's mother came into the room. "What are you going to write to your pen pal about?"

"Help me, Mom. I have no ideas."

"Tell her your name, about the family, your school, where we live, and what it's like. Then she'll probably say the same about her, and things will pick up from there."

Glumly, Sam wrote:

Dear Sally,

My name is Sam Riley, and I live in Nebraska. Having a pen pal was my teacher's idea, and everyone in the class has one. My family is made of my mother and father, older sister Peggy, and my little brother Mitch. My birthday is August 21. What is California like? Nebraska is very flat, and there is a lot of farming going on here. Do you have hills? I play the piano and the saxophone, my sister plays the flute, and my little brother tries very hard to play the trumpet. We have a lot of fun jamming sometimes. Do you play an instrument? I also like basketball and writing stories. What other things do you do?

> Your friend,
> Sam

It was only a week later when he got a reply. Sally wrote:

Dear Sam,

Thank you for your letter. My mother said I should have a pen pal because I am too shy around people. So she thought that a friend I can't see would help me get over my shyness.

> Your friend,
> Sally
> PS, my birthday is April 1.

Sam was confused. She said really nothing about herself, so how was he supposed to write her again? He mentally hiked himself up and wrote:

Dear Sally,

Thank you for your letter. You really didn't say anything about yourself, and I would like to hear from you. What do you like to do? Where does your family go on vacation? Do you have any brothers or sisters? You know, things like that. Thank you for sending me your birthday. My teacher will add it to all the other pen pal birthdays.

> Your friend,
> Sam

It took Sally three or four letters before Sam was able to get the vital statistics from her. She loved horses, she was the only child, and she lived with her mother. Her teacher's name was Mrs. Feldman, and she liked the idea of a pen pal. She also played the flute like Peggy and wrote stories like Sam. She wanted to be an author when she grew up.

Sam took it from there. By December, they were having a lively exchange; and finally, Sam suggested that they swap pictures which could be their Christmas presents to each other. Sally readily agreed but warned Sam that she didn't take a good picture. Sam didn't care. He wanted to see what this girl he didn't want to write to at first looked like. Sam sent her his class picture.

When he received Sally's picture, he sat down. Hard. She was beautiful with light blond hair, sunny blue eyes, and a shy smile. For the first time in his life, Sam was in love.

He didn't quite know what to do with his feelings, so he just kept it to himself. He was anxious to know what Sally thought of his picture. When she replied, he was not disappointed but also not thrilled. She said he "looked like a Sam," whatever that meant.

But Sam really didn't care, and he bought a frame for two dollars, same as the cost of the pen pal service, and put Sally's picture in it on his desk. He looked at it all the time. He never told even little Mitch what Sally meant to him, and certainly not Sally!

After the year was up, it was up to each one in the class if they would continue writing. Most of them didn't, but Sam didn't want to let Sally go, so the correspondence continued between California and Nebraska.

Just before seventh grade started, Sam went to the old oak tree in the park in town. He gently whittled away some bark and carved their initials in the tree on the side that was mostly out of view.

Sally and Sam continued to write through high school, but during the college years, they seemed to float apart and eventually lost touch with each other. Sam had several girlfriends during that time including one named Sally. But it was that faithful heart of his stayed with the girl whose initials and his were on The Tree.

1956: THE PRIZE

Henry was so glad he finally bought a television. He wasn't too happy with the money he had to spend, but at least, he didn't have to call friends to find a place where he could watch his favorite show, *The $64,000 Question*. He also had the feeling his friends were getting rather tired of entertaining him.

Henry was an editor with a textbook publisher. Although he liked his job and could take manuscripts home and learned a great deal from them, he was more or less stuck in town. He envied his friend George who worked for a candy company and got to go to exotic places like New York and Omaha for meetings.

Henry realized George should be home from his latest foray into New York and was about to call him for news on his latest adventure when his doorbell rang. It was George. They traded greetings, and Henry asked him about his trip.

"Henry, buddy, you're not going to believe what happened this trip! I got tickets for *The $64,000 Question*, and I went and saw everything. I thought of you and wondered if you could even stand it. It was that exciting. I know how fond of that show you are."

"You really got to see it in the studio?"

"Yep, and I have more good news. My company is having a "Bring a Friend to a Convention" week so others can get a taste of what I do. So I signed you up, buddy. We're going to New York!"

"Sorry, George, but I just can't afford that. Think of someone else to take."

"Almost the best part of the deal is the company will be paying for the whole thing. You know, airfare, hotel, food, and the like."

"You said 'almost the best part.' What did you leave out?"

"The very best part is that I got two tickets to *The $64,000 Question* for the second night we'll be there. How about that, old buddy?"

Speechless, Henry just gaped at George. What a pal to include him in the chance of a lifetime!

"Henry? Henry! You all right? You look a little pale."

Henry snapped out of his surprise. "Yeah. I'm fine. I just can't believe it."

"You still have to go to the convention, but I don't think you'll mind. It's wall-to-wall candy, with as much as you can eat, all you want. It's booth after booth after booth, everyone encouraging you to take a sample. But as a newbie, I have to warn you not to eat too much, or you will get sick. We can't have you too sick to go to the television studio."

George's words meant nothing to him. All he could see in front of his eyes was that television show practically in his lap. He was quite overwhelmed.

It was the longest two weeks Henry could remember, but, as it does, the days passed in due time; and George and Henry winged skyward. When they landed at New York's Idlewild Airport, he was overwhelmed by the scope of what he saw.

"Don't worry, Henry. I'm an old hand at this, and I know how to get us where we want to be."

It seemed only an instant before he and George were at the convention hall. Henry was sure it was four–football fields large. They met with a few of George's friends and their guests and then started booth hopping. Henry, who thought if he could stand his own cooking, considered himself blessed with an iron stomach. With all that candy, he did what George predicted. The next day, he was much choosier.

The second night was *the* night, and Henry, who had eaten very little at the convention that day, was up for it. In fact, in the cab on the way to the studio, he wanted to bounce up and down like a kid.

Inside the studio, it was a mass of people talking and laughing, some shouting, and the band tuning their instruments getting ready to play the theme song. Henry had no idea it would be this much of a mess. When he was finally able to sit down, he looked ahead at the stage and saw those familiar things he saw on his TV: places for the isolation booths, the "Revlon" sign, and lo and behold, he caught a view of Hal March, the emcee.

The crowd settled down suddenly when the announcer came out and instructed the audience when to applaud and when to say a disappointed "aww" which was practiced.

Then he asked if anyone in the audience would like to become a contestant. Henry couldn't believe himself when he raised his hand.

He was taken backstage to leave his name and phone number. He would be contacted by phone for an interview since he lived so far away.

Back at his seat, George just stared at him. Henry just shrugged and put on a grin that nothing could wipe away.

It wasn't for several weeks until the show called for the interview. Apparently, he passed it because they asked him to come to New York for a further meeting. He was about to say no and that it was out of his price range when the associate producer added that the plane fare and the hotel would be on their bill. How could he say no?

In New York, he was met by an aide to the producer and a limo that whipped them off to the studio. Henry didn't like all the bustle. He decided New York was not his favorite place.

He was interviewed by an associate to the producer.

"Mr. Matthews, may I address you by your first name?"

"Sure," Henry answered, unconcerned.

"Well, then, Hank, let's—"

"Excuse me, but the name is Henry."

"Then Henry it shall be. Let's start with a few easy questions and work up to the more, shall we say *entangled* questions, shall we?"

Henry smiled expectantly. They went through with some elementary questions in his chosen category, The American Presidency. Reading and editing all those textbooks and their facts was finally coming to flower.

"And here we go with the last one. You're doing very well, but this is a toughie. Remember to think before you speak. Who was the first president to be born a US citizen? All previous presidents had been born under British rule."

"I know that, actually," Henry said confidently. "I learned that in sixth grade. It was Martin Van Buren. As an added bonus, I'll tell you he grew up speaking Dutch, not English."

After that, it was a rush of various offices, papers to sign, and people talking to him about he didn't know what. It was all a wonderful blur. He was told, however, that there was a surplus of contestants at the moment, and it may be weeks before he was called to come back to New York.

Strangely enough, the call came two weeks later. He was told that some contestants had backed out, not an unusual event, so they were ready for him.

A week later in New York, he was actually *in makeup*, so he would present himself on television as *a regular guy*, something he found terribly amusing. His hair was restyled, and he was handed a new suit. Henry felt like he had lost who he was. But he got a grip on his identity and found himself waiting in the wings for his name to be announced. *Was he nervous?* he asked himself. No, not really. He didn't mind speaking in public, but he just tried not to think of the millions of television viewers. That would make him nervous.

When he was announced, he put all his energy into the history of the presidents while trying to be charming for the viewers. Charming actually won.

His first question was so elementary that he almost laughed when he heard it: "How many children did George Washington have?"

With all confidence, he simply said the right answer. "George Washington had no children." The audience burst into applause. And so, Henry won a dollar. Every time he answered a question correctly, the amount would double until he got to $64,000.

"And will you come back next week and try for two dollars?" the emcee asked.

"Of course, I will," Henry replied. Huge applause met that statement.

When he got to the Omaha airport, there was a crowd there to meet him, his church group, his neighbors, and a few people he didn't know. However, he didn't see George.

And so it went, week after week, Henry continued his upward odyssey to the top prize. After so long, only a volunteer driver met him at the Omaha airport, and the rest of the town did a lot of waving when he got home. He wasn't such a novelty anymore.

He studied his books at home, and good thing. The questions were getting much harder. He was asked things like, "In a single hand of poker, what president lost the White House China?" Of course, he answered correctly: Warren G. Harding. In a question just two weeks ago, he was asked, "Who was the only bachelor ever elected president? It was duck soup to Henry: James Buchanan. He was almost bored with the game.

But he had one more question to go before he would be a $64,000 winner. All that money! He was going to have so much fun with it in addition to buying a new car and a new house.

The night of the show he was in good spirits. He went through makeup, again; but this time, they left his clothes and hair alone. The show's staff had taught him how to appear well-dressed on his own.

Henry could feel the audience's tension when he stepped into the isolation booth. He had Maurice Albright, a history professor at a local university as his expert. Henry asked Maurice because he was an old friend, not because he needed his advice. He was ready.

The question? *Too easy*, he thought. "There were two First Ladies with the name Abigail. Who were they?"

Henry didn't have to think, but he was told he had to appear nervous so tension build in the audience to make it more exciting. Then he appeared to whisper something to Maurice who appeared to whisper back. They nodded at each other.

When called for an answer, he said, "The two First Ladies with the name Abigail were Adams—"

"That's correct," said the emcee. "What was the other one?"

Henry paused to build tension. "The other First Lady was Abigail Fillmore."

Henry didn't expect an explosion, but he had one! The audience went wild, the band played, and everyone seemed mad with joy!

The next day, with a check for $64,000 dollars in his suitcase, he arrived in Omaha, expecting nothing more than someone to drive him home. But there was the high school marching band, half the student body, the faculty, the church choir, and his entire neighborhood. It was the studio audience all over again.

But George wasn't there.

Henry had had no time for George with the studying, catching planes, the hubbub behind stage, not to mention his job. But Henry was sure George had understood the pressure he was under. However, just to make sure, he telephoned George. No answer. Henry thought he would catch him later.

As that thought was passing through his mind, the doorbell interrupted his reverie. Of all people, it was George!

"Hey, buddy, I just tried calling you. You must have been on your way over here," Henry said extending his right hand for a friendly shake.

"Hey, Henry," he said without enthusiasm or making an attempt to take his outstretched hand.

"Well, come on in! I have some coffee on the stove, but I think I can scare up a whisp of brandy." Henry paused for George to answer, but he was silent with a rather despondent look on his face.

"George, what's the matter? I haven't seen you in weeks, and you show up with this forlorn face? C'mon, we're buddies. You can tell me anything."

Finally, George spoke. "It's that money. That's a lot of money, and everybody knows you have it. How are you going to manage all that wealth?"

I'm going to put most of it in the bank and use some of it for a new house and a new car. Did you know my old Chevy is a '46? It's an old car now. And this house is a dump. But why do you ask?"

"I had a cousin who inherited a huge plie from his dad when he died, and the idiot went out and told everyone. He also bought a new car and new house, and he kept spending, lending people he hardly knew money, then bought a business in Grand Island. He thought he could make even more money."

"What's wrong with that?"

"His business went under, he lost thousands in the loans that no one repaid, and he didn't consider that he had to report his income to the IRS."

"What happened to him?"

He lost every friend he thought he had. He was stuck with so much inventory he couldn't sell that he ended up donating it to Goodwill, which deepened his loss, and he was in deep yogurt with the income tax people."

"Where is he now? Is he still around?"

"Oh, he's around. Around about ten years in the slammer. Henry, I don't want to see that happen to you! I came here just to give you that warning and to say that I'll be around, but probably not here as I know firsthand how money can change a person. Do yourself a favor: Don't buy a new house, fix this one up. Don't buy a new car, buy a used. It'll cost a lot less, and you won't go putting on airs with it."

"Why are you telling me all this?" Henry asked, completely overwhelmed.

"Because I'm your friend, and I don't want to see you go down."

"I'll be fine!" Henry said with confidence. "You know me. Old rock-solid me. Nothing like that is going to happen here. Your cousin was just a spendthrift."

"Yes, that, and he is an idiot."

Henry laughed, but he lost the merriment as soon as he looked into George's eyes. George was dead serious.

George, still unsmiling, said, "I don't think I'll be coming around for a while. Not until you have settled down off that high the TV show put you on and get all that money in the bank. I don't want to see my good friend go down in smoke." With that, George turned, went out, and slammed the door behind him.

"Ridiculous," Henry muttered. But there must be a grain of truth in it if he had already lost a friend before the first cent was spent.

Although Henry got the money to the bank, he kept out a few thousand to have around the house. He hid it in the pages of the Encyclopedia Britannica's volumes.

The next morning, the phone rang just before eight o'clock.

The phone rang while Henry was dressing for work, and he picked it up. It was Don Winkles, one of the accountants at the publishing firm.

"Henry," he said with a very serious note in his voice, "don't go spending even a penny of that money until you talk to me."

He sounded like George.

"You have to pay taxes on that dough, and it will be a lot. Let me help you figure it out."

Henry thought it was a splendid idea. He wasn't about to end up in Leavenworth.

At work, he gave all the necessary information to Don; and later in the day, Don came by Henry's office. It was a huge chunk of money.

"But that won't leave me enough to buy the house I want, much less the car. How can they take that much away from me?"

"Because they're the government, that's why."

In the days to come, Henry received many surprises, none of them good. He got calls and people at his door begging for money. They wanted a loan or a donation. Henry didn't even know most of these people, and the ones he did he found them exceedingly rude. He was even starting to receive calls from all over the United States. He finally called the phone company and asked for a new number. It didn't work. They still called. Henry was at his wit's end.

After a few weeks of that kind of treatment, Henry became a hermit. He only went out of his house to go to work. Most of his friends stopped talking to him anyway, calling him a snob for not filling their monetary needs.

He had to get rid of the money. He could spend what was left! But in the end, he realized it wouldn't get his friends back, and the phone would still be ringing. He put what he could afford into the bank where he wouldn't touch it. Then he could falsely tell everyone he was out of funds. But he figured they wouldn't believe him. He had put a substantial amount in the bank, but he still had thousands of dollars in cash hidden in his house. That was making him nervous.

Whenever he was troubled, he used to go to the park in the square and sit with The Tree. It was time he did it again. The tranquility was what let him think, but that day, it was far from tranquil. It was Saturday, and the park was crowded with little kids and their mothers, big kids and their bikes, and older adults with their pigeon food. Henry figured that if he could get an idea with chaos around him, it would have to be a good idea.

He walked to the back of The Tree, leaned against it, and sighed.

I've set aside enough money to fix up the house and buy a newer car, Henry thought. *It's all the leftover money that's raining havoc on my life. Everyone wants me to loan them two thousand dollars here and five hundred dollars there. But then there are the ones that expect me to donate to every charity on the planet. I just wish I could throw this cursed money away!*

Henry turned around and leaned against the tree. His head hit something on the tree that he was unfamiliar with. He lifted his head and turned around. Brushing a branch away, he saw a plaque. Whipping out his glasses, he was able to read the weatherworn print that declared The Tree was at least five hundred years old, and the town had grown around it. It also mentioned that no one knew how it got there. He also noticed that one of the screws in a corner was missing. Pulling the corner out, he saw a big empty behind it. Henry began to laugh!

That night, when the town had settled down, and most were in bed, he dressed in all black, took his leftover money, and went to The Tree. He carefully unscrewed the other three screws holding the plaque over the hole. Then Henry took a thousand dollars at a time and stuffed it in the hole the plaque had covered. As he saw the bill go fluttering down, he began to giggle. The more money, the harder he laughed. Still chortling, he stuffed the last of the money into the hole and carefully replaced the three screws.

Now, he thought, *someone would have to cut down this tree in order to find the money, and I suspect it will happen one day. But it's gone from me, and I'll get my friends back, and life can go on the way it was before I won that cursed stuff! I hope whoever claims it has the sense to tell no one about the find.*

Henry went home that night and stuck his television set on the back porch. He had no use for it now.

And he laughed!

1977: THE VISITOR

It wasn't that she didn't like doctors, it's just that Molly was sure she would know if something was wrong with her. A doctor wouldn't know if she had pain, an infection, or heart problems before she did. She thought it was a waste of time since having yearly checkups. If there was something wrong, it was easy enough to find by herself. Then she would let the doctor know.

The previous Wednesday night after choir practice, Molly had gone down the side steps to the parking lot as she had at least a thousand times before. However, this time, it was different. It was dark, and she caught the second step with just her heel, and down the three steps she went, landing on her right knee. Except for skinning that knee, Molly was fine. After being helped to her feet by two other choir members, she brushed herself off and declared herself fit. She went home.

On waking the next morning, there was a stiffness in her leg that Molly had never felt before; and when she tried to get out of bed, her right knee wouldn't hold her, and she collapsed. Molly called for her husband, Ed, who came out of the bathroom with shaving cream half on and half off. When Ed saw Molly's knee, his face became the same color as his shaving cream, prompting her to look also. It was the ugliest, blackest, and bluest spread she had ever seen. Ed wanted to take her to the ER, but she said an emphatic no. Molly tried to get up again and moaned the whole way up. She needed Ed's arm to walk. This didn't sit well with her.

"At least let me call Dr. Heimerkoner and get you in right away."

"His name is 'Kohnheimer'. And for a change, yes, I recognize that I need his help."

"Hallelujah! She's seen the light!"

"Just call. No need for a gloat."

According to the doctor, it was a minor thing. It just looked worse than it was, but the doctor advised she get herself a pair of crutches and sit down as much as she could with an ice pack on her knee.

"As long as you're here," Dr. Kohnheimer said, "I want you to get a mammogram. You're overdue, and I happen to know you can get in this morning."

That didn't sit well with Molly. Every week, she examined herself just as the pamphlet the doctor had given her had prescribed. She would have known if there was something wrong. Maybe. She consented in spite of her skepticism.

After the mammogram, the technician asked Molly to wait for a few minutes. That was odd. She had never had to wait before. To her surprise, she was then taken to another room with a table and told to lie facedown while they took a sample of her tissue. Molly was getting more and more worried.

Dr. Kohnheimer called her that evening. He was very short.

"You have cancer."

Molly was glad she was sitting down.

"What, uh, what do I do? I don't, I mean I can't—"

"The first things I need you to do are to call Dr. Malloy to be the surgeon. I also recommend Dr. Tobias. I would like to see you use him as your plastic surgeon. You'll have to have a mastectomy and call right away. It's small now, but it's fast-moving cancer. So the sooner, the better."

"Will I have to have chemo?" Molly could barely ask.

"No telling about that until after the surgery. Right now, I'm going to arrange with the hospital for an OR within the next week. Please tell that to the surgeons so they can arrange their schedules. Got a pencil? I'll give you their numbers."

Molly made pantomime movements to Ed, and he grabbed something to write on. He took down the numbers Molly dictated.

It was all happening too fast. The next day, she found herself in Dr. Malloy's exam room who explained everything to her. By this time, Molly was shaking on the inside, angry on the outside. Her weekly breast self-exams hadn't done any good. And it took a doctor to tell her she had cancer, not the other way around as she had always said.

On the way home, she parked the car by the town square and went to visit The Tree. It was always there for her. Solid, almost kindly, she thought about all the things The Tree had been through in its enormously long lifetime, and it always made her troubles feel just a little less.

Six days later, Molly kissed Ed and was walked into the OR where she would lose a part of her sexual identity. She was afraid Ed wouldn't love her anymore now that she would be damaged goods. But she and Ed had such a good relationship. Maybe, just maybe.

Molly thought she saw a light, so she opened her eyes just a bit, and the first thing she saw was Ed smiling at her. She tried to smile back, but she hurt so much that she couldn't keep it up. She retreated into sleep again.

The next time Molly woke, Ed wasn't there, but the nurse said he had gone to get some dinner. Dinner? Molly remembered she had gone into surgery in the early morning. What was going on? Sleep won.

Again, Molly woke. Ed was there, and it was very dark outside.

She tried to speak, but she could only croak out her question. "How long?"

Ed came over to the side of the bed. "You were in surgery for nine hours."

"I'll bet the doctor's feet hurt," Molly managed to get out.

Molly had an urge to touch herself to find out what was done and where most of the pain was coming from. The exertion was just too much, and the drugs made sure she would just rest as much as possible.

Ed was there, and it appeared to be dawn. Molly felt strangely rested. She opened her eyes all the way and looked around. The room was without decorations and was sterile looking. She didn't care.

Suspicious, Molly asked her husband, "How long have you been here?"

"I slept here last night."

"Why?"

"I just wanted to be here if you needed me."

Just then, the nurse came in with a cup, and Molly could hear ice chips jiggling as she walked.

"You need to start putting something in your stomach. This is just water, but you're dehydrated, so it is important you drink all of it."

Molly hated ice water. The ice hit her sensitive teeth, and the temperature of the water actually hurt. She rejected the offering. "No ice, please." The nurse was quick to comply. Molly had to admit that the water was more than welcome; she drained the cup and asked for more, please.

A simple liquid diet was added the next day. Molly hated Jell-O, but there it was on her tray almost daring her to eat it. She enjoyed the hot soup and the ginger ale but left the Jell-O alone.

After a day and a half, Molly was moved from that sterile-smothering room to a regular hospital room with a spectacular view of the roof next door. It didn't pick up her spirits, but at least, she was allowed food from a special menu. She wasn't really hungry, ignored the menu they gave her, and picked up her book. Even reading was difficult as she had to use her arms and hands to hold it. It wasn't easy. And every time she had to use the toilet, she had to have someone with her as her knee was still in charge of moving around.

On her third day there, her pastor came to visit. Pastor Susan was an angel, and she was cherished by the congregation. The two of them had a lively conversation about water sports. In the back of her mind, she realized that her favorite sport, swimming, was going to be out of her realm from now on.

Ed was always coming and going when his schedule would allow. He showed up early on the fourth day with something behind his back. Molly's first guess was flowers, but she was wrong. He brought her tree branches with leaves on them.

"What is this, Ed?" She inquired anxiously.

"Branches," he replied. "Don't you just love them?"

"Why should I?"

"Because, my dear wife, they are branches from The Tree. I know how you love The Tree. And since you can't go to The Tree, The Tree is—"

"Coming to me," she finished his sentence. "I couldn't ask for a nicer gift! But The Tree is protected. Isn't it against the law to take the branches?"

"No need to tell anyone. I did it in the wee hours when no one was around, and they're only very small branches. See? Just big oak leaves on a stick. They won't be missed." She smiled, hugged the branches he gave her, and told him where to find a vase. In her mind, no flowers could outshine The Tree leaves. It was a lovely gesture, and knowing that it was from The Tree made her feel just a tad better. But the blues had set in, and she couldn't shake them. Even being told that she wouldn't need chemo didn't seem to warm her heart.

Every night, around two in the morning, a nurse came around to take her vitals. They would tiptoe in turning on the dimmest light in the room so Molly would barely awake as the cuff squeezed her arm. Then they would go away, and Molly would fall right back to sleep.

On the fifth night, Molly vaguely heard the nurse coming in. Instead of turning on the dim light in the corner, she flicked on the big one over her bed. Molly opened her eyes and saw a diminutive figure in scrubs. This wasn't Harriet, the nurse who had introduced herself at shift change.

"Hi! My name is Julie, and I'm your nurse this evening."

"What about Harriet? I thought she was my nurse."

"Harriet is busy with a bunch of patients that came in late," Julie explained. "Seeing patients like you is what I do best."

Molly couldn't help but notice that Julie was entirely bald with a flimsy scarf failing at an attempt to hide her pate.

"I can see you noticed my head. I had a double mastectomy about three weeks ago, and this is from the chemo."

Molly was astounded. "Aren't you going back to work a little early? Shouldn't you give yourself some more recovery time?"

Julie laughed. "What? Stay home and watch television? I live for patients like you. I love my job. And they thought since I went through what you did, I could be the most help. So I was sent."

"I have to give it to you." Molly felt as if Julie was warming up a very cold soul.

"Like I said, I do best with patients like you."

They talked for how long Molly couldn't tell, but Julie was easy to talk to, and they discussed all sorts of things. It wasn't until Molly glanced out the window and saw the dawn she told Julie to get back to work. "I'm sure you have others to visit."

"Actually," Julie said in her warm and easy way, "I don't. You were the only one on my list."

Molly was hard put to let Julie go. This wonderful nurse had taken a burden off of her and made her future look much brighter.

When they waved goodbye, Molly realized that Julie never took her vitals.

Molly never did get back to sleep. She was actually excited for her future. She looked at the branches and leaves from The Tree. Just the sight of them brought her calm and courage. And Julie was a part of that.

She couldn't stop thinking of the things she discussed with Julie and how she enjoyed her company. She decided to ask Harriet when Julie would be on duty next. Maybe she could get in another long conversation.

Harriet came in about seven o'clock with another nurse.

"Molly, this is Mandy. I'm going off shift, and Mandy will take over for me."

They exchanged hellos.

Molly just had to ask. "Harriet, can you tell me when Julie will be on duty again? I'd love to see her before I go home."

"Julie, you say?"

Molly nodded.

"We don't have anyone on staff named Julie."

1985: THE WEED

Earl had been told he was stubborn. And he admitted he was but only about things that mattered. He was also told he was grumpy, secretive, and conniving. He was sure he wasn't. He told himself that he wasn't grumpy, secretive, and conniving; he was serious, private, and clever. *Ah!* he thought, *those who called him those names could go fly a kite!*

One rainy day, a seed got washed into a crack between the neighbor's cement walkway and the side of the garage. It began to grow. Earl saw the weed shooting up and grumbled that if it were his, he'd go pull it out straight away. Instead, he censored the thought, and the weed just got bigger and bigger. Earl was disgusted because he was scrupulous about his yard and kept all weeds out. But no, this bungler kept missing it, and it was now too big to pull. It needed to be chopped out. Earl had to almost sit on his hands so he didn't go over to his neighbor and complain. He didn't want to be called rude also. But he couldn't get the weed out by himself on someone else's property. So it grew.

The weed was obnoxiously visible from Earl's kitchen window, and it grew bigger each year until it was twenty feet high. It had several trunks, each mothering many long, sweeping branches. According to Earl, it was about as ugly as a weed could be. And it dropped seeds: little helicopters that ended up on his lawn.

His neighbor had no interest in getting rid of it. In fact, he called a tree service to enhance the health of the weed, and they ended up cutting off one of the trunks. *At least that was something,* Earl thought. But from his kitchen window, all he could still see was that obnoxious weed.

It was windy the next day when he went out to mow the lawn. As he passed the weed, the wind whipped the weed's branches, and one of them went smack in Earl's eyes. That was all Earl needed. He went into his garage and got his tools and began to saw and clip the tree. It was intoxicating! About then, his neighbor came over and wanted to know just what Earl thought he was doing.

"Just clipping off what is on my property. It's something the law says I can do. I won't hurt your precious weed more than a trimming."

"It's a tree," the neighbor countered with conviction.

"Did you plant this thing?"

"No," the neighbor admitted.

"Why would you allow a weed that planted itself to grow in your gutter? It's also going to compromise the concrete floor in your garage."

"It's a tree, it's mine, and I'll deal with it." The neighbor stomped away.

"And they call me stubborn," Earl said under his breath.

But that wasn't the end of it. He had to get rid of that weed.

He thought of just continuing his *trimming*, but the neighbor was too alert to what Earl was doing. So that wouldn't work. He thought of damming off the drainpipe so it would curtail the weed's water supply. No good. The neighbor would see the dam and take it down. He'd have to think about that for a while.

He had errands to run, so he put those thoughts aside. He drove to the village square, parked his car not far from The Tree, and set off for the bank, the menswear store, the auto parts store, and the diner where he stopped for some talk and a cup of coffee.

Earl ran into the same group with whom he usually had coffee, and it was almost a novelty to see waving, welcoming hands and invitations to join them. What's new, they all wanted to know, just like they wanted to know every time. Earl thought it was a good crowd with whom to let off a little steam, and he spilled the story about the weed.

"I would have just kept chopping and, oops! Sorry, the ax slipped and chopped off that big trunk," one of his friends said.

"Yeah," another advised, "then he'd have the law on Earl. I have a feeling you would rather not have that happen, right, Earl?"

Earl nodded. "I'd appreciate your suggestions. How can I get rid of a weed that's now about thirty feet high with half of it hanging over my roof? I can cut off the leaves on the bottom, but I have no way to get at those tall, heavy, threatening limbs. Guys, I really need your thoughts!"

"Why don't you get a tree service to come in and take the big ones down for you?"

Amazed that such a suggestion was even an option, Earl answered, "Do you have any idea what that kinda service costs? Would you pay four hundred dollars for that? Even though a third of the tree is legally on my side of the property, they guy probably wouldn't do it anyway. Besides, I'd have to call a *weed* service, not a tree service."

Earl sighed, finished his coffee, and left the shop. Instead of going right to his car, he detoured to The Tree and sat down with his back to the tree. He reached behind him and patted the ancient trunk.

"Well, Old Boy," he said softly, "you didn't have this kind of trouble when you were growing up. There was no one around to trim your branches. No one wanted to end your life. But what was it that would have done you in? No water? Bad water? A tornado? Bugs?"

Earl sighed, sat back, and thought. *I've tried the no-water option. That didn't work. We have no real bad water, just once we had to boil our drinking water. I couldn't direct a tornado to hit it, and I have no idea nor resources to find out what kind of bugs would hurt it. What do you think, Old Tree, old friend?*

It wasn't more than a few seconds when Earl felt a tapping on his soul. He listened, and a voice said, "Bad water, the wind, and bugs."

No, he thought, *that wasn't anything I heard. I was just thinking about those things. I have no control over any of them. But if I could, what a dead weed it would be!*

Earl went to bed that night with those things on his mind. There was no way! He had no control over any of them. Or did he? The Tree had spoken. Or had it?

The first thing Earl did the next morning after he got dressed was to go into his crowded garage to look for the herbicide he had bought several years ago. He found it, but it looked so ominous that he put it aside for the time being.

After breakfast, he used the last of the pancake batter and flapped a few more jacks which he then covered in syrup. He let them sit until they soaked up all the surgery goodness, broke them into pieces, went outside, and put them around the base of the weed.

"This'll attract every sugar-loving insect around," he said to himself. He could visualize an army of irritating ants, wood-chopping beetles, and wasps building nests. To encourage ants to climb higher, he even put some pancake in a place where the crux of a branch split into three almost out of his reach. He wiped the syrup from his fingers on the leaves.

He left the weed alone to give the insects a chance to discover the cache for themselves. When he went back two hours later, he didn't see pancake pieces covered in ants. In fact, he saw no pancakes at all. What he did see was a squirrel sitting and staring expectantly at him with a "What's up, Doc?" look on his face.

Okay, bugs were out. And he had no control over the wind.

So it would be the herbicide. It was time for the only thing he had left.

He quickly made sure the neighbor's cars were gone, and then he dumped half the jug of herbicide on the main trunk and watched it as the weed sucked it up.

In the days and weeks to follow, he gleefully noticed a definite change in the weed. The leaves turned brown, rolled up, and fell off. What was left of the dangling branches that had smacked him in the face stiffened and, when a gust of wind came along, they broke off.

A few weeks later, there again was the tree service truck out in front of his neighbor's house. Earl was almost beside himself: That weed was going! What he found, though, was only two-thirds of the weed was taken down. The rest was left. And Earl noted that it was any part of the tree that was on his property.

"I give up, Earl," his neighbor shouted at him from the back of his house. "You win. You can have your part of the tree."

Earl was stunned. "Hey, get that service back and come have them take the whole thing down," he shouted back.

"Can't do that. It's not on my property." His neighbor went inside and slammed the door.

Earl couldn't remember ever being so angry! And he could do nothing. All that was left was the hulking ghost of what used to be the weed.

Two nights later, he sat out on his deck, still burning with anger. He felt a lovely breeze, but a flash caught his eye. He looked west and saw a leviathan black cloud heading straight toward his area. However, he didn't run inside. He liked thunderstorms and liked to watch them come up. He would know the best time to run for cover.

The wind picked up. Hard. The black cloud was still far enough away that he was encouraged to stay and watch. He saw debris being blown between the houses, and one of his lightweight lawn chairs was skittering across the deck.

Then he heard it. There was a thunderous crack and a huge gust of wind. He was sure the immediate following crash was heard by the whole neighborhood.

The last trunk of the weed had been picked up and thrown on Earl's house, shattering through the roof.

Just like a tree.

PRESENT: THE ASSIGNMENT

New to the town, Marilee O'Hara was fascinated with The Tree. It was her first teaching assignment, and she felt she was bursting with ideas for her soon-to-be fourth-grade class. She had gathered a lot of history of the town and The Tree and hoped to use it in her teaching. And she was quite surprised that there was so much history in such a little town with a big tree.

Wondering why The Tree seemed to be the only arboreal oak around, she began to ask questions of the people. Everyone knew The Tree, and everyone had an opinion on how it came to be. Some of the stories were out-and-out whoppers while others were carefully thought-out explanations. All were about as different as one oak is to another. She also noted that The Tree didn't have a name. It was just "The Tree." It seemed to satisfy everyone, so Marilee left that alone.

When school started in September, she found out what being the new teacher on the block was all about. Just out of teacher's college, Marilee was barraged with advice from every teacher in the school. It wasn't dictatorial advice. Marilee was sure it was "just the way things had always been done." But she had other ideas and was going to try several lasting assignments that would be ongoing all year. The other teachers lost their smiles when they heard this, and a few clucked their tongues and shook their heads. "New teachers always think they know how to teach," was the buzzword among the staff. "Give her a bit of time, and she'll find out that our ways are best."

Marilee caught wind of this and thought, *But your ways are dull and out of date. Mine is the new day.*

The first day of school was exciting. Marilee knew how to watch for the leaders and see that they weren't leading the class in the wrong direction. Wally was the leader who was not averse to standing up at his desk in the back of the room and making hooting or other annoying repertoires. Apparently, each outburst made sense to the others in the class, so Wally was greeted with laughter and a bit of hooting themselves. She had to get Wally on her side at once.

She explained to the class what would be ongoing in their class in the next year. The class responded with, "Oh, Ms. O'Hara, that sounds boring," and "Do we have to?" And from Wally speaking with great dignity and an English accent, "I don't know if I want to do that," followed by giggles.

"You'll find out when you do these assignments, and I'll be happy to help anyone. You will have a new awareness of not only the English language but of a whole new world around you."

"No, I won't," Wally said in a warning voice without even raising his hand.

Ignoring Wally, Marilee began to write on the board the crux of the assignment. "You all know a word that has three double letters in it. Can anyone tell me what that word might be?"

Silence. Finally, Nina, a diminutive girl in the third row, raised her hand and said, "Mississippi?"

"Right!" Here is your assignment, and it will last for a month so you have plenty of time to find as many triple-letter words as you can, keep a list, and the one who has the most triple-letter words will receive a prize."

"Ms. O'Hara," said Shane, one of Wally's compadres, "where are we going to find those words?"

"Ask your parents, an older brother or sister, your grandfather or grandmother, read as many things as you can. You'll be surprised how many of those words you use all the time and never thought about it. You all have one word to start out with, so when you get home tonight, you can begin."

And so the year went. From month-long project to month-long project, she watched her students' enthusiasm grow with each new assignment. Marilee was delighted and surprised to find that three times Shane had the title of most of whatever that month's assignment. Wally even stopped challenging her.

She had the best saved for last.

"You are all familiar, I'm sure, of the old oak tree in the town square park."

Everyone nodded.

"But think about it for a minute. That tree is ancient. It's estimated to be five to six hundred years old and still healthy. That in itself is amazing. So who can tell me what important event happened when the tree was only about a hundred years old? Think way back to the beginnings of American history when no one but the Native Americans lived here."

There was silence. Then slowly three or four hands went up, and she called on Talisha.

"The Tree was here before Columbus discovered America?" she asked.

"Right, Talisha! Do you know what that era was called? I know you all know it."

No hands went up this time.

"Remember what Talisha said that it was here before?"

"I know! I know!" Wally volunteered.

Marilee tried not to show her astonishment. "What do you think, Wally?"

"It's pre-Columbus," he said proudly.

"Close. It's pre-Columbian. Good one, Wally."

Wally actually surprised Marilee by being a very good student and consistently got *A*'s and *B*'s. But for some reason, he didn't want anyone else to know about it. So he put up a tough exterior to keep anyone else from getting too close to him except for Shane and two others from another class. Instead of looking proud of himself for his mostly correct answer, he slumped back in his chair and gave off a look of defiance.

"So here's another thing to think about The Tree. It's been around for a long time, it's an oak tree where there are no other oak trees around for at least a hundred miles, and it took root on an empty plain. How did it get there? Where did it come from? Did a Native American plant it? Did it arrive here by accident? Were there any of the native animals involved? Did Mother Nature have a hand in it? This is your assignment. There is nothing to study or look up. No one really has the story, so maybe you can think up your own story. Use your imagination but make it a real possibility. No fairies, witches, spacemen, or the like are invited. You can ask others, but what you turn your assignment into me has to be your own idea. Have fun with it, go visit The Tree, see how much the town depends on it. Think of all the things The Tree must have seen."

There was the usual sound of sighs that came with any assignment, but Marilee also heard an undeniable note of excitement in the underlying whispers. She had to congratulate herself. This was going to be a good one. However, she noted, for the first time, Wally was scowling and slapped his hand on his desk in frustration. She didn't know what to make of it.

Before the last day of school, all The Tree assignments were in, and some of them were thoughtful, and some of them were imaginative while still others showed a lot of logic. Wally's was flawless, and for what Marilee knew of The Tree, he had the best explanation. Why he flared up at first was still a puzzle.

On the last day of school, there was a lot of whispering going on, and Marilee pounced on Roberta, the class gossip.

"Are you talking to Meg about The Tree assignment?" she asked knowingly.

"Yes, Ms. O'Hara."

"Class has begun. Tree talk will come later."

"We were just wondering what kind of a prize you'll be giving out on the last assignment. We think it should be very nice."

"It is, but that's later, not now."

Roberta nudged Meg and grinned at Marilee.

The kids were all restless that morning, and the afternoon was even worse until Marilee finally decided it was time to end class.

"Okay, class," Marilee said clapping her hands to get their sparse attention. "It's now time for The Tree assignment."

That got their attention.

"In order to properly finish this assignment, we have to take a field trip."

This met with excited buzzing.

"Let me point out that there are no winners or losers this time, but to properly reveal some of the answers, we're going to have to honor The Tree with our presence. I mailed all your parents permission slips, and they have signed and returned them. I wanted this to be a surprise for you on this last day."

Everyone was excited, even Wally appeared to be looking forward to the trip. The walk was a short one, up a block and over two. They all sat down under The Tree and, much to Merilee's surprise, were quiet.

"I'm going to hand back your papers to you, and you will see no grade. All were winners. When I call your name, will you please stand up and read your paper. We don't have time for all the papers, just a few. Let's start with Roberta."

Roberta was obviously tickled to be the first, and she loved an audience.

"There once was an acorn," she read, "that had no place to go. It was on the floor of a forest that was crowded with other oak trees, and there wasn't a chance that it would be planted. But one day, an Indian…oops, sorry, I mean 'Native American' was out gathering acorns, and he picked up the lonely one. The man began to walk, and he walked a very long time and for many days. Then one day, the sky turned black, and a huge storm blew the acorns out of his pouch, and they were on the ground. It rained on them and they sprouted. Only one survived, and that is The Tree in our park."

That girl is going to be a gossip columnist one day, Marilee thought.

"Thank you, Roberta. Wally, it's your turn."

Wally looked at her with a mixture of disbelief and determination.

"The Tree was born from an acorn that a bird ate while it was migrating. While he was flying over what is now our town, he pooped, and the acorn was caught up in a tornado and was drilled into the ground and was planted."

The class fell over laughing, and Wally grinned.

There's a future senator if I ever heard one, Marilee thought.

"I thought it was a very interesting perspective on the scenario, Wally, though I think you could have worded that another way. It's perfectly possible that is the way that it happened."

"We have time for one more. Paige, how about you?"

There was nothing shy about Paige, and she was smart as a whip. She stood up and read her paper. "A squirrel was living in one of the trees one hundred miles away. He dropped the seed and then a herd of deer came along. They kind of kicked it away. It stayed there overnight, and then a mouse picked it up. A hungry owl picked up the mouse. On the way to the owl's nest, the mouse dropped the seed. It rolled a bit into a stream. It floated on the water for a while, and then it caught on a rock. It stayed there for a few hours. Then a Native American picked it up and put it in his bag. He was walking for a few miles, and the seed fell out of the bag because there was a hole in it. Then there was a storm. Lightning hit the ground near the seed and caused soil to cover the seed. And then…bam! The baby oak was born."

That girl is going to be famous for her storytelling! Marilee mused.

"Thank you, Paige, for your imaginative telling. Did all of you hear all the reasons? What do they all have in common? Who can tell me?"

"It wasn't planted by people," Mia said.

"Right, but how did it get planted?"

"By the weather," Donnie shouted from the back.

"That's right, Donnie," Marilee said in surprise. Donnie never volunteered for any answer. "And that's how Mother Nature intended it to be. Not everything was a cause of weather, but in this case, these three people agreed. Just a bunch of you said The Tree was planted by squirrels or rabbits but didn't tell us how the acorn got to be one hundred miles from the other oaks. The point of this assignment was to have fun, use your imaginations."

"Then who's the winner? What's the prize?" asked Shane.

You are all winners! As for the prize, turn around, and you'll see."

Heads turned, and they saw a man with enough helium balloons to lift him skyward.

"Oh, neat!"

"Cool!"

"All for us?"

"Best prize of all!"

Marilee walked over to the vendor who handed her some of the balloons. "I want each of you to take one and hold on to it. When I give the signal, we all let go as a tribute to The Tree."

Excitedly, each one got a balloon, some jostling for their favorite color, and then stood expectantly waiting.

A gust of wind came up just as she was about to give the signal.

"Let them fly!" Marilee yelled as she let her own balloon go.

They were carried up and twisted in the wind. The balloon belonging to Wally flew up and got caught in The Tree, and he grinned as if he had planned it. When they were out of sight, the class relaxed; and finally, someone asked what time it was.

"My goodness," their teacher said, "it's almost four o'clock! School has been out for almost an hour. Quick, run back to school, pack up your belongings, and have a wonderful summer!"

Everyone except one person made a beeline for the school. Marilee stopped to talk to him. It was Wally.

"Wally, don't you want to get your summer started?" Marilee asked.

"Aw, I just wanted to say something to you."

"What is it?"

"Thank you," he said and kissed her on the cheek. "If you tell anyone I did that, I'll deny it my whole life." Then he ran off.

"At least I did something right," she said to herself with a sigh. She looked at the sky and the tiny dots high above dancing in the wind. The benches around The Tree looked so inviting she couldn't help herself.

"Here we are, my friend, and here I'll stay. We just sent your next generation flying. I wish I could see all the things that have happened to you, and I can't wait to see what happens to you in our years to come."

ABOUT THE AUTHOR

 Wife, mother, grandma, world traveler, and bibliophile, Kathleen Olson lives in northeast Illinois with Tom, her husband of fifty-six years. Also sharing the Olson household are two cats, Goober, and Piper, who are the ones who really run the house. As a child, Kathleen saw the crosscut of an old tree where the rings told the story of it going back before Columbus. She thought of all the things that could have happened around that tree and what could become of it. Happily, the result was The Time Tree which she proudly offers to you.